GW00888878

Never Be Closing

The 7 Essentials for Inspired Sales Success

Never Be Closing

The 7 Essentials for Inspired Sales Success

by

Ted McGrath

Hardback ISBN 978-0-557-39799-0

Paperback ISBN 978-0-557-35411-5

Acknowledgments

To my brother Tucker, who inspired me to be better;

To my mentor Moe Abdou, who taught me to be the best;

To my Mom and Dad, who blessed me with the rest and to Phil Tanzillo for your expertise and Inspiration behind this book.

Live Inspired,

Ted McGrath

Overview

A talented group of people wakes up in the middle of the night scared and restless. These are the millions of sales professionals wondering where all the money and all the clients have gone. Are you one of those people?

"New and daunting research has revealed that 40 percent of sales professionals/entrepreneurs aren't even meeting their basic quotas."

Let's face it; a 40 percent decrease means depressed sales people, depressed businesses and a depressed economy. In business:

Nothing happens until someone sells something.
If there is nothing sold, a business does not exist.

It's time for the revival of the sales professional and not just a revival, but also a transformation.

Never Be Closing is for Sales Professionals seeking an "edge" in the competitive world of business or Sales Professionals Seeking Peek Performance.

It's not enough to be a sales professional today; you must be a sales entrepreneur. I call it the "Salespreneur" - someone who creates value by crystallizing the desires and vision of his customer and takes sole responsibility for inspiring a customer to take action NOW.

Being great isn't enough today. You must be outstanding and companies won't stand for or survive on anything less.

The purpose of this book is crystal clear: generating immediate income for you as a sales entrepreneur. Throughout this book you will learn time tested principles and the most cutting edge sales processes in the world for increasing your sales and INSPIRING your clients to TAKE ACTION NOW. You will become a master at helping clients clarify what they want and you will gain revolutionary insights into the driving forces behind WHY clients buy. *Never Be Closing* will be a key stepping stone to providing you with the lifestyle and income you have always dreamed of, the ideal clients you have always imagined, and the client relationships that make for a fulfilling and purposeful life.

The processes and principles I share with you have been handed down to me from my mentor of 25 years in sales and entrepreneurship. At 21 years old, I made a six-figure income as a salespreneur using and applying these principles and processes. For seven years, I was a partner and a leader of 120 sales entrepreneurs in the New York Life, Orlando General Office - one of the most successful offices for the #1 life insurance company in America, a multi-billion dollar company. My role as the #5 Partner (out of 500 Partners at New York Life) was to hire leading edge sales professionals, teach them how to build a business and show them how to sell in a high pressure, commission-only environment. Our sales people had a very small window of opportunity to make it or FAIL. The year I left, the last four people I hired ALL made $40,000 in commissions their first month in the insurance business. Why did I leave? A HIGHER CALLING. For the last four years (coming up on 11 years as a Sales Entrepreneur) I have been teaching *Never Be Closing* across the world.

You know what they say, if you can sell insurance, you can sell anything. I believe that the answers to your higher calling in sales are in this book.

Never Be Closing: The 7 Essentials for Inspired Sales Success

Chapter 1: The Secret to Unwavering Confidence in a Sales Situation

Chapter 2: Get 90% of Your Results Before you Show Up to the Meeting

Chapter 3: The Mystery Behind Why Some Clients Buy and Others Walk

Chapter 4: Communication That Flat Out Sells

Chapter 5: The Opening Sales Conversation for Immediate Results

Chapter 6: Turning Thousand Dollar Customers into Hundred Thousand Dollar Customers

Chapter 7: Transforming Objections into Assets

What makes *Never Be Closing* totally different than anything else out there? Answer: the way you live and the way you impact your customer's life.

Traditional sales people live in their world.
A Salespreneur lives in his/her client's world.

Traditional sales people sell, influence, persuade and CLOSE their clients into their world of products and services. A salespreneur understands, appreciates and INSPIRES his/her client's world to make his/her client's desires and vision a reality. There is nothing wrong with sales and influence – a salespreneur works with them too. The difference is how you define it and if you are comfortable being what you define. *Never Be Closing* is not about who you *become* in a client situation, it is about who you *are* in all situations.

- A Traditional sales person closes the deal.
- A Salespreneur Inspires their client to take action.

- A Traditional sales person sells products and services.
- A Salespreneur sells a desire and a vision.

- A Traditional sales person changes a life situation.
- A Salespreneur changes a life.

Which one are you? Or who do you want to be?

A salespreneur knows one thing for certain that a traditional sales professional does not know. A sale is not about closing, it is about inspiring your clients to action. In fact, ABC ("Always be closing") is an outdated paradigm that dies with the traditional sales professional. "Always be closing" will fade from your awareness as you go further and further along the journey of becoming a salespreneur.

I invite you to the new world of the salespreneur: NEVER BE CLOSING. *Never be closing* is not a statement, nor is it a lesson. It is a philosophy, a new way of thinking, a new way of being for the new world sales professional, now known to you as the salespreneur. Flowing from every word, chapter and process in this book is the new world of sales; a new world simply because outstanding people don't want to be closed, they want to be inspired to take action. Inspire is what you do as a salepreneur. Every new process in this book will lead you to inspire your clients to take massive action and you will never be closing again.

"Waste no more time talking about great souls and how they should be, become one yourself."
- Marcus Aurelius

Your life is about to change. Read on!

Welcome to the beginning of your Education in "Never Be Closing"

"The only thing that I see that is distinctly different about me is that I'm not afraid to die on a treadmill. You might have more talent than me, you might be smarter than me but if we get on the treadmill together, there are two things: you're getting off first or I'm gonna die! It's really that simple. I have a ridiculously, sickening work ethic." – Will Smith

IT IS THE BEST OF TIMES.... – Charles Dickens

I start this book with two quotes: One from the famous actor Will Smith and the other, a modified version of the famous quote from, A Tale of Two Cities, by Charles Dickens. The two combined will set the precedence for what you are about to experience in this book.

Yes, this is a book on sales, but this is more than just a book. It is the beginning of your DEFINITE commitment to being the BEST in your trade. If you are reading this, the odds are you "sell" to others for a living. My question for you is, "Are you ready to be the best?" Being the BEST is a commitment to rise above the standards that have been set for you; it means you set a new standard that has never been set before. Being the best means you do not get off the treadmill. When things seem difficult or challenging to you, you keep going and going and going. You learn and master the tools I share with you throughout this book. I expect the BEST out of you, just as I have given you my best in writing this masterpiece for you. It's not just a sales book, it is a symphony. When you learn all the notes, the melodies and the tunes in this book, you will begin to create your own masterpiece.

IT IS THE BEST OF TIMES. Facing challenging times? Bring your best. Have a tough client? Bring your best. In a down economy? Bring your best. Having a bad month? Bring Your Best! The only thing you see and stand for is "The Best of Times" in every area of your life. That's what you look for, that's what you create and that's what you *represent*. Together we will accept nothing less. Together you and I will co-create the most magnificent sales practice you have ever dreamed of. Are you willing to bring your BEST? The time has arrived. Be your best self NOW. Be Your Best Sales NOW!

I mentioned my work with the New York Life Insurance Company. At 21 years old I was the # 4 producer out of 120 Financial

Advisors in my office. I made six figures in income my first year in the business. Was I the best sales person in the office? No. Was I the most talented in the office? No. Was I the most skilled in the office? No. There was only one thing that made me one of the top superstars in that office: a commitment to being the BEST. My boss had an expectation and demanded that I be the BEST. In return I committed to work long hours, practice relentlessly and never settle for anything less than my BEST. That commitment is what led me to the MASTERY of the sales processes that I share with you in this book. AND, I can assure you, theses processes are the BEST!

Do you know what I discovered in the last 11 years? Without confidence and a belief that you can be BEST, nothing else matters. I promise I will share some incredible processes to help you generate immediate revenue in your business, but before we jump into those waters, make a commitment to really diving into the exercises in Chapter 1 - "The Secret to Unwavering Confidence in a Sales Situation." I know it's tempting to go right for the sales tools and processes, but these tools on confidence are going to make you lethal in a sales situation.

Before we begin I have two questions for you:

1) Why did hanging out with strippers every night for 2 ½ years make The Beatles the greatest rock band ever?
2) Why was Bill Gates destined for greatness at age 6?

The answer is simple: The Ten Thousand Hour Rule. Malcolm Gladwell is the author of the bestselling book, *Outliers*. In his book he shares three very important pieces of information that explain how to become a master or expert in anything. He is the author of the "Ten Thousand Hour Rule."

The Ten Thousand Hour Rule

1) To become an expert in something, it takes 10,000 hours of practice.
2) 10,000 hrs = 3 hrs/day x 10 yrs.
3) There are no prodigies.

It's possible that you too could spend 2 ½ years, 7 nights a week and 7 to 8 hours a night with strippers. That's what The Beatles did. They played over in Hamburg, Germany every night at the strip joints for 2 ½ years and they became the greatest band that ever lived. After putting in their 10,000 hours, they came to the U.S. and released what became their first platinum record. Before they went over to Germany, it was said that they were a good band. They went from good to BEST in a short period of time.

The good news is, to become a master as a salespreneur, there is a simpler formula. The next piece of news is good or bad depending on your preference. There are no prodigies, only people who master their craft and their skill. For most people the formula is 2-3 hours per day for 10 years and they put in their 10,000 hours. I spent the first seven of my 11 years in sales, mastering my process from 8a.m. - 9 p.m. at night. All day long I was selling to clients; training others to sell to their clients; or selling my financial advisors on their own future. I have become a master in sales and inspiring clients into action. It is not at all what I thought it would be. When you become a master in an area, you gain a different appreciation for what you do. It becomes an Art and every day is about painting your masterpiece. For the last four years I have been preparing and practicing and waiting for the day that I could bring my masterpiece to the entire world. Today and every day that someone reads this book is the beginning of my new journey, a journey to help you become a master in the new world of salespreneurs.

Bill Gates started his Ten Thousand Hour journey at six years old in a computer lab. It's no wonder that ten years later he dropped out of college with a vision to "have a computer on every desktop across the world." Masters change the world. Masters commit to being the BEST. IT IS THE BEST OF TIMES. BE YOUR BEST SELF NOW!

"Two roads diverged in a wood and I... I took the one less traveled by and that has made all the difference." - Robert Frost

"I will do today what others will not do, so tomorrow I can do what others cannot do." - Randy Gage

Table of Contents

Introduction

Have you ever seen the movie *Patch Adams* with Robin Williams? In the movie Robin Williams plays the character of Patch Adams, who admits himself to a mental hospital because he is depressed and has lost his inspiration for life. In the mental hospital he realizes the doctors aren't there to relate to the patients; they are just there to diagnose. They don't even connect with the patients; they just analyze their charts. Patch Adams has a moment of inspiration where he connects with his mentally ill roommate and helps him overcome paranoia. When he truly connects with his roommate, he realizes he has a higher calling in life, he realizes he truly wants to help people and he enrolls to become a doctor.

On the first day of class, the Chief of Staff M.D. comes out and gives a speech that scares the crap out of the incoming students. The incoming students don't know what to make of it so they clap in a state of confusion. Part of them knows that what the M.D. said was flat out WRONG, yet they completely deny that part of themselves. The other part of them feels pressured to conform because this is the way it's always been done and the M.D., who is revered as the expert, says so. They accept what the doctor says. After all, God forbid they question the M.D.

Here is the speech from the M.D.: "The sad fact is human beings are not worthy of trust. It is human nature to lie, take short cuts, to lose your nerve, get tired, and make mistakes. No rational patient would put his trust in a human being and we're not gonna let him. It is our mission here to rigorously and ruthlessly train the humanity out of you and make you into something better. WE'RE GONNA MAKE DOCTORS OUT OF YOU."

In this moment, Patch Adams realizes that there is something fundamentally wrong with the way doctors are practicing medicine. This isn't to say that they are doing a bad job. It's simply to say that they could be doing so much better. They could be more understanding, appreciating, relating, connecting and inspiring to help their clients get better.

Friends I feel the same way about the sales industry. Something is fundamentally wrong with the industry philosophy. Somehow the statement, "we're gonna make doctors out of you" mirrors the sales industry mantra, "were gonna make closers out of you." Or maybe it's better known to you as "Always Be Closing." Somewhere along the way we lost our humanity and began to believe that a doctor or a sales person was above being human. As if we have a special power to decide the fate of human beings.

I believe you have been drawn to this book because you realize there is something deeper to the human spirit. That something deeper is knowing that patients don't want to be operated on any more than clients want to be closed. They both deserve to be TREATED with compassion, empathy and a sense of humanity. They are human beings and being an incredible doctor or being an amazing sales person is just that, being human. I would encourage you in this book to not turn your back on what you hear inside yourself, to not turn away from your conscience. Rather, embrace the higher power for which the salespreneur was meant to serve: inspiration, my friends, inspiration. And with that, I welcome you to *Never Be Closing*.

I was 22 years old. It was my second year in the insurance business. Every morning at 5 a.m., I went to the RDV sports complex in Orlando, Florida. I lifted weights for 45 minutes, read my book on the treadmill for 30 minutes and took a cold shower before getting my hustle on for the day. After my shower I would throw on my custom made Armani Suit and drive off in the new Mercedes that I had just purchased. Life was grand and so was the money!

What was the purpose of my life at the time? To make lots of money, to have lots of fun and to experience "the good life." I had never experienced life like this before.

To think, one year earlier I was sleeping on a mattress in a house with five other guys and eating the *Uncle Ben's Rice* that had been sitting there since the last tenants moved out. And then one day it happened; THE CLIENT came to me.

Many of us sales people work our whole lives for the day the clients will come to us. We pray and we work, we work and we pray, for just that moment. All the days of waking up, putting in that extra effort and looking the part, we believe will one day work out; or at least we HOPE.

On this particular day – when "THE CLIENT" came to me – I didn't know it would be the greatest lesson I would ever learn.

My brother and I worked out together at the gym. The client and his brother also worked out at the same gym. My brother and I would see them at the gym every morning and soon we all became friends. During all that time we never approached them for business. Well, the time had come and they approached us. The irony was that the clients first approached my brother and then my brother passed them along to me. And that was the day I started to learn the real principles and lessons of business. For the first time, I was confronted with an option: I could be a "Sales Person" or I could be a "Salespreneur."

What did I decide?

I knew in my heart that the right thing to do was to take them through a process that would crystallize their desires and help them create a vision for their future that could be magnificent. I knew how to help them. I had been trained and prepared for this moment. But when I shared our process with THE CLIENT, all he really wanted was for me to take the order. I couldn't believe it. This was the moment I had been waiting for, my dream client and he didn't even want to explore the possibilities. He just wanted me to take the order and invest his million dollars. In fact, he didn't even have me meet his brother. He just wanted his brother to invest his money as well.

I couldn't understand it. I knew that just taking the order wouldn't do the job for them. I knew that I wouldn't be putting my best foot forward if I couldn't give them a holistic view of their life and their planning. I knew I would just be selling a product and I wouldn't be any different than anyone else out there. I knew in that moment that business had become something less than what I had dreamed it was. I knew that somewhere along the way, the sales profession had lost something, or MAYBE IT WAS NEVER THERE TO BEGIN WITH.

And you know what? I took the order!!!!

Was I right or was I wrong?

Did these clients help me advance in my career? Did they help put incredible money in my pocket? Did they go on to invest 20 million dollars with me four years later? Yes, yes and yes they did. (You read it right: they invested 20 million dollars with me.)

Now for my final question: Was the client relationship fulfilling?

No it was not. I traded a fulfilling relationship for money. I love both of these guys to death, but in the end, the situation was one of the biggest headaches I had ever dealt with in business. I wasn't a "salespreneur" to them. I wasn't a person who helped them with their deepest desires and their life's vision. I was a "sales person." I was an order taker and that's how they treated me.

I received countless phone calls from one of the brothers, yelling at me when the market would go down even one point. Every day at the gym I would go hoping not to run into that one brother. The quality of my days was being decided by the fluctuation of a product and the mood of a client. Did I ever establish the business rapport that is necessary with clients? Did I truly connect with them beyond the deal? Did I help them with anything in business other than taking an order?

NO, NO and NO!

Truth be told, I wasn't strong enough to stand my ground. Perhaps this was destiny and it was a lesson I had to learn to be here now sharing with you. I'm not condemning myself for taking the order, yet I am highlighting it as a lesson of how not to live a career and a life as a sales person. We learn from mistakes and we also see the good in them. And from there we decide who and what we want to be.

In retrospect, I know now I wouldn't trade that experience for the world. I learned and matured a lot during that time AND I will never do it again. Now I know I'm not willing to trade my principles, my beliefs, my integrity, my dignity, or my self-respect for "THE CLIENT" that we all hope for. Sometimes "The Ideal Client" is the very client that turns out to be "NO DEAL." Or at least, not the deal you truly deserve as a SALESPRENEUR.

I'm not saying you won't make mistakes. I'm not saying you won't have poor judgment at times.

What I am saying is, make a mistake once, shame on you. Make the same mistake twice and it could turn into a business nightmare.

Look at my example. Not only did I make the mistake on the first million dollars. I could have turned it around and stood my ground the second time for the 20 million dollars and I didn't. My second mistake had 20 times the magnitude. I should have stood by my principles and insisted they go through a process that would not only benefit them but would establish the ground rules for mutual respect in our relationship. Instead, I learned that if you don't, the client can make up anything he wants and fly by his own set of rules and expectations and that's what happened to me. They called and said, "Jump!" and I said, "How about off the 29th floor of my office building?" When someone gives you 20 million dollars, it comes with a set of expectations, trust me.

So the first thing to do is decide whom you want to be right now. Do you want to be an order taker or do you want to be a "salespreneur?" I know it's tempting, when the money comes up, to take the order. In the end, I made great money with these clients, but it wasn't the life I wanted to live and it wasn't the business I had always dreamed to build. You will have your own experiences and you will learn from them just as I did. Then you will make your own decisions of what path is right for you.

The lesson here is this: if I never took the order I might never have learned the lesson. Each one of us chooses a path to learn the paradoxes of life: the hot, the cold; the good, the bad; the right, the wrong. In the end, who is really to judge? Maybe we can learn to appreciate it all and simply learn to improve it.

I recently watched an interview on 60 Minutes with Katie Couric and Andre Agassi, former tennis champion. Andre just wrote a book called Open where he reveals his deepest and darkest secrets. In the interview with Katie, he actually reveals that years ago he used a drug called crystal meth and he secretly hated tennis his entire life. He was driven by his dad from the time he was a young boy. By the age of five he was practicing six to seven hours per day. His dad had a special ball machine built that shot balls out at 110 miles per hour. He was only a small boy at the time and that's when his secret life began. He lived with this secret hatred of tennis for years. That's right, he claims he hated it. Finally at 27 years old when he began using drugs and his tennis game hit rock bottom, he made a decision in his life. After years of hating tennis and feeling like the life he was living wasn't his, he made a decision to choose tennis and to choose to be great and appreciate the sport. At 27 Andre made one of the greatest comebacks in the history of sports, becoming one of five people to win all the major championships and was ranked #1 in the world again. I want to leave you with Andre's quote as we venture into this book. "I learned to appreciate tennis because the thing I hated, led me to my wife Steffi." Tennis led Andre to marry the # 1 women's tennis player in the world, Steffi Graff. The thing he hated led him to the happiest years of his life with Steffi. Life does have a sense of humor, doesn't it?

Isn't it amazing how some of life's greatest treasures are often hidden? *Never Be Closing* is one of those treasures. It's right here in front of us, yet it is hidden in an industry that has lost itself in the fog. It only becomes clear when we decide and choose to live our careers in an inspired way. When we begin to give meaning and appreciate the people and gifts that are in front of us, the world opens itself up for our excellence as human beings to shine through.

Here are the questions I would like you to answer on your journey into the world of the salespreneur.

- Who are you?
- Why do you do what you do?
- What's your purpose?

Take a moment to answer these questions now and see how you evolve and how they evolve throughout this book.

Once you can answer these questions and *live by the answers you give*, I know the best salespreneur in you will emerge. Life or business isn't about who you are in the simple moments; it's about who you become in the challenging moments. Those moments define your business and they define your life.

"You can only become truly accomplished at something you love. Don't make money your goal. Instead, pursue the things you love doing and then do them so well that people can't take their eyes off you." - Maya Angelou

Chapter 1

The Secret to Unwavering Confidence in a Sales Situation

"Increase your confidence and you will increase your sales." - Ted McGrath

"I've missed more than 9000 shots in my career. I've lost almost 300 games. Twenty-six times, I've been trusted to take the game winning shot and missed. I've failed over and over and over again in my life. And that is why I succeed." - Michael Jordan

What is the Secret to Unwavering Confidence in a Sales Situation?

Michael Jordan was definitely one of the most confident athletes I have ever seen. One thing I learned over the years is that successful people model other successful people. Ask yourself, what made Michael Jordan as confident as he was? Why did they always give the ball to Michael for the game winning shot?

Michael Jordan had a process for making the game winning shot. He took the game winning shot 10,000 times in his mind before he actually took the physical shot in a game. He visualized making that shot over and over again until he was certain and 100% confident that he could make it. He developed a systematic process for greater confidence and results. This is why Michael Jordan knew when he stepped on the court he was going to succeed.

Most sales professionals believe that prospecting is the key to success in their trade. Sorry to break the news - are you ready for this? - sales people don't call on new customers because they lack the confidence. Prospecting isn't the key to success, confidence is. Lack of success for sales people doesn't just come from a lack of confidence in the product, it stems from a lack of confidence in them selves. Increase your confidence and you will increase your sales. Increase your confidence and you will never have a shortage of new people to call on again!!!!! A confident person is a magnet for attraction. A salespreneur is confident and values confidence above all things. It is your greatest asset! Protect it like its gold. If you're not confident, nothing else matters.

Did Michael ever miss a game winning shot? Yes! As a matter of fact, he missed twenty-six game winning shots and over 9,000 other shots in his career. But here is what we learn from great people such as Michael Jordan: success isn't always about winning the game, it's about having the confidence to take the shots.

Wayne Gretzky once said, "You miss 100% of the shots you don't take." I am asking you, the salespreneur, to take your shots. I want you to develop the confidence to take the shots that even seem impossible. Greatness lies in doing the impossible.

Let's get straight to the point here. In this chapter I share with you seven confidence builders for incredible success in sales. What is a confidence builder? It's a process or a ritual that helps build your confidence before or during a sales meeting by putting you in a powerful and resourceful mental state for success. I think you would agree that having the right mindset before and during a client meeting is critical to success, wouldn't you? The selling mindset is fueled by confidence.

Although, you can't just rely on a powerful mindset to bring results, you must have a mental process that delivers systematic results. Throughout this book I share many processes to help you get predictable and systematic results. When you learn these processes, do you think that you will be more confident? Absolutely. In a moment you are going to develop you own processes for success. You will also learn that the key to succeeding with these processes is mastering the art form behind selling.

Confidence comes from a mastery and appreciation of the selling process. There are certain skills that you must learn along the way as a salespreneur. Once you learn these skills and practice them over and over again, you won't just be a sales person; you will be a Master in Sales and Influence. You will understand what true artists appreciate when they create a masterpiece. Your masterpiece, your Mona Lisa, will be helping your customers' desires and dreams become a reality.

"Do the thing you fear to do and keep on doing it... that is the quickest and surest way ever yet discovered to conquer fear."
- Dale Carnegie

Confidence Builder #1: NBC - Never Be Closing

"You don't ever have to close a client; you just have to inspire him into action." - Ted McGrath

You are most likely familiar with the famous phrase ALWAYS BE CLOSING. Many people also refer to it as "ABC". If you look back to all the great movies in history that involve sales, you will hear this mantra over and over and over - Always Be Closing. In the famous movie, "Boiler Room" with Ben Affleck, he has an entire scene on ABC where a bunch of ego driven, testosterone filled guys are all pumped up to close their next deal and make the big bucks. Ben Affleck pumps up the new recruits by ranting about being a "fucking millionaire, driving a Ferrari and being totally liquid."

The crazy thing is that sales people have gotten off on this for years. It has been embedded in our entire culture of sales and our entire existence as sales people. "Boiler Room" is somewhat a mirror of the famous film "Glengarry Glen Ross," a 1992 independent film, adapted by David Mamet. The movie covers two days in the lives of four real estate agents and how they become desperate when the corporate office sends a representative to motivate them. The "motivating" speech is delivered by Alec Baldwin, the company's top sales man. He berates the non-performers and proceeds to drill into their psyche our famous sales mantra, "Always Be Closing."

As a sales person, it's easy to get swept up in this type of thinking. Its forceful, it's "motivational" and it's driven home with such certainty by its messengers. After all, if "ABC" made it to Hollywood than it has to be true. And come on, we don't want to be seen as wimps in the office who aren't closing deals. There is no room for non-performers in this world. We won't settle for it and as time moves forward and things speed up, you either perform or you're out.

Well, some of this is true AND only SOME of it. It is true that we must perform or we don't advance. This is the truth of the world. However, I would ask you to reconsider your entire perspective and viewpoint on the world of sales if ABC happens to be your mantra.

Perhaps it is your mantra and maybe it isn't. Maybe you were attracted to this book because you always sensed that something wasn't right with ABC. Perhaps you were using this philosophy and mantra on a day to day basis and you never really felt like it was REAL. By

REAL I mean, true and authentic to who you are. Did you really get in business to CLOSE your customer? Is your life's work about Always Be Closing and always treating the customer like a scorecard rather than a person? I don't think that is you. In fact, I don't think anyone intends to be THAT.

And still, from time to time, we follow a philosophy or mantra and we live our life by a set of rules that we have never even questioned the validity of. We just assume it to be REAL because everyone else is doing it.

I wrote this book because in the last 11 years, I knew the purpose of a sales professional to be completely different. I knew that as a salespreneur who is evolved, compassionate and authentic, that Always Be Closing is completely outdated and has been for quite some time and you knew it too. You sensed it, didn't you?

And I am guilty of following the ABC model in the past. From time to time my mind has wandered off the person/client in front of me and has focused on what I need to do to close the deal.

But what I learned was simple: I could never be passionate about something that didn't give me the opportunity to develop passionate and authentic relationships. That's why I left the insurance industry. I wasn't passionate about my life and my relationship with my clients anymore. I realized that ancient mantra ABC was not what sales was about. I was fortunate to have a mentor who taught me well and never subscribed to the ABC mentality.

As all courses run their path, ABC has most certainly run its path. Its time is over. It has served its purpose. It trained many people to sell many things and it has brought us into an era where we must now question the very principles of outdated business practices. It's time for new principles and new leaders in the world of sales. I have elected to be a spokesperson for the next generation. And what I have to say is "NBC- Never Be Closing".

I am introducing a new era in thought; a transformation for the sales professional and a revolution in the sales industry. Mark my words: "No one is against the ABC fans, it is just time for an upgrade into the NEW world." Your clients want it, your peers want it and you want it. We have been begging and pleading for something new. Something, so we can go home at the end of the day and feel passionate again, feel real again, feel inspired again and that's exactly it. Never, ever close a client again! All you have to do is inspire them into action and these are all the principles and the processes you will learn in this book. You will learn revolutionary processes that completely change the game and the world of sales. It's no longer a game, it's an art form. A freakin' Mona Lisa! And you are part of the transformation! You are leading the revolution with me. Are you ready? Let's dive into this a bit more.

I know this goes against the grain of all the sales books and techniques out there and I am still going to insist on this Confidence Builder: "Never BE Closing". You don't ever have to close a client; you just have to inspire him into action. Strong arming doesn't work. Clients will buy when they are ready. It's okay to get them ready and to give them a directive on what the action steps are and it's okay to influence them; just don't close them.

Why shouldn't I close people?

Have you looked at the dictionary definition of "close"? It means "to deny access to". This is just one of the definitions. I am aware "close" has other meanings too, however, I don't even want to use language that means or resembles denying access to something.

But let's make it personal. Who are you being when you are closing people? How would you feel if you walked into buy a car and you overheard the sales man say, "I'm going to close this guy today." How do you feel when you know someone is trying to "close the deal" and he's not in tune with your desires and feelings?

What if I told you, you actually make less money with "closing" and that I can teach you how to make ten to 100 times more money without closing?

Never Be Closing! Instead of "closing", inspire people into action.

Definition of Inspire:

1) To affect, guide, or arouse
2) To fill with enlivening or exalting emotion
3) To stimulate to action; motivate
4) To affect or touch
5) To draw forth; elicit or arouse

Try saying to yourself, "I am going to inspire this person into action today," how does that feel?

Change your language and change the meaning you give to certain things and you will change the quality of your entire life. When you change the language or the meaning of something it changes the emotions and feelings you have about that particular situation. When your emotions change, your experience and quality of life changes. Imagine how "inspiring" will change your experience of the client meeting and as a result how your client's experience with you will change.

You have all heard the word "influence". Would you like to know my definition of influence? Actually, I created two new meanings:

1) Influence: To inspire people, you must figure out what already inspires them.
2) Influence: Put other peoples' desires before your own and in the end both your desires will be met.

What if I told you that when you inspire clients, they will take action faster, they will tell more people about you and you will make more money? It's the truth.

Who are you being when you are inspiring people? Authentic and real. You are being your Best Self. I say Be Your Best Self NOW. Will you go into your client meetings now with more confidence because you are being the real, authentic you? Absolutely.

You're probably wondering, "Ted, how confident or certain are you that your hypothesis *Never Be Closing* is correct? Are you sure this is the best or most effective course of action?"

I am sure, I am positive and I actually KNOW that *Never Be Closing* is the new path for the new world salesprenuer. Sometimes we just KNOW and you KNOW it too, don't you? However, don't just rely on my knowing. Experience it for yourself and test all the processes that I introduce to you in this book.

We will talk in later chapters about language and communication that inspires your clients into action, so that you will NEVER BE CLOSING AGAIN.

Activity:

1) Before your next client meeting, list one thing you admire about your next potential client. It's hard to close someone when you actually admire him. When you admire someone, you will want to inspire him and you will bring your best self to the meeting.

2) Describe a time when you purchased a product and you felt you got great value. What inspired you to buy this product and how did you FEEL during the process? How many people did you talk to about your experience and why?

Confidence Builder # 2: The Art of Questioning

"Judge a man by his questions, rather than his answers." - Voltaire

Why is it important to ask questions during your client meetings?

a) The Quality of the Question Determines the Quality of the Relationship.

The depth of your questions actually shows the depth of your understanding of a clients' situation or problem. When you understand the depth of your clients' concerns and desires, how much confidence do you think you will have in recommending the best possible solution? You will be extremely confident because you were willing to go deep with your clients and they will appreciate how astute and conscientious you are.

b) Shift From Selling to Questioning.

As a salesprenuer you have to make the shift from selling to questioning. For most sales people this is a pretty big paradigm shift.

We have been trained by the industry to "Sell! Sell! Sell!" In fact, it is programmed in our brains to throw it up all over a person from the moment we meet him and start telling him all the benefits of our products. Maybe someone should change the name of "Sales" to "Questioning". Then "sales people" would become "question people" and they would have more satisfied clients. The point here is that when you ask the right questions you give your client the opportunity to BUY rather than be SOLD. This is a big difference.

Activity:

Let me share with you one of the most powerful questions on the planet: What do you want? Take a moment and answer the question. List five things you want right now. Be clear and specific.

My example:

1) To be passionate every day of my life
2) To be happy for the rest of my life
3) To write a bestselling book
4) To speak in front of 10,000 people
5) To have an enjoyable meal tonight

Your example:

1)

2)

3)

4)

5)

After doing this exercise, what do you notice? I wrote down some things I didn't even know I wanted. I knew I wanted my book published but I wasn't consciously aware that I actually wanted a bestseller. I also wasn't thinking that I wanted an enjoyable meal tonight.

c) <u>You Aren't Selling to your Customers, You are Unleashing Their Potential</u>

The question, "What do you want?" helped bring out the potential in my life. A question brings into existence something that wasn't clear or conscious only moments ago. Your questions will bring your clients' random thoughts into clear, concise and specific thoughts that now have direction and passion behind them. What a gift for you to give to someone!

Let's examine the power of this for a moment. You're probably thinking this question – What do you want? - is the most basic question on the planet. It is and it isn't. Ask a simple question and sometimes you may not get a simple answer. The bottom line is many people don't know what they want, or they never take the time to consider what they want. This question will bring your client right into the moment. It is so simple that he must come up with an answer that is clear and concise. To do that, he must be present to what is going on in his life.

I use this question in an opening conversation with a client over coffee. I've devoted an entire chapter to the opening conversation with a client. I don't use the information I receive to sell the customer like many people do. I use the information to understand my customer. There is a difference. Many sales people use information as ammunition to collect and then fire back at their clients to close them or they never bother to gather the ammunition because they never ask a question and they just shoot their own ammunition. Either way the ammunition kills the connection with the client. You should follow the approach of understanding your customer. The more you understand them, the more you will ask them questions that lead them to owning their solution to their problem or to their opportunity. When a client answers the question, "What do you want?" it:

1) Tells you where they're at.
2) Helps you understand who they are.

Now that you know who they are and where they're at, you can begin to get your client to start owning what it is they want. How can someone own what they want before they know what they want? When they own what they want they will be inspired to take action on what you can give them. When they own it, you can give and they will buy. What I just said may require you to read it more than once as it is profound.

You could say that when I ask this question, I am still in the exploring phase of the conversation. As you will see in later chapters, I don't just ask this question when I show up to the meeting. I can easily inject this question into a casual conversation.

The secret to asking great questions is to make it seem like it is part of the natural conversation. A great salespreneur feeds off the conversation and looks for the right opportunity to ask the right questions. A good question should be seamlessly integrated into your meeting. So Mr. Client, it sounds like things are going really well in your life, "What else do you want these days?"

It doesn't matter whether they have exactly what they want right now. Human beings always want more. You ask a question and that question puts us into our "creator mode." The brain says, "What can I create for my life today?" And if you get someone into a conversation where they are comfortable and the dialogue is flowing and they are doing most of the talking and they are on a roll, they will be able to answer that question as a "creator." Then all you have to do as a salespreneur is continue to create with them. You become their co-creator.

We will talk about how to really be effective with questions later on. In Chapter 3 I get into uncovering someone's driving needs! You will love it. This is totally new to the sales industry. No one is using the content in Chapter 3 the way I am using it and the way you will be using it.

Just thinking about your profession differently and changing how you talk about things will change your entire business. It will ignite your passion. When you know that every meeting is about unleashing someone's potential by asking questions, how much confidence will you have going into that meeting?

d) <u>The Right Questions Result in the Client's Buying</u>

How does questioning result in your client's buying?

Most people would rather die than think. Most sales people would rather die than ask questions. If you're still selling in a world that doesn't like selling then you are in trouble. The irony is that sales people like to sell. People often equate selling with talking. Sales people talk. The problem is that the old methods of selling by talking are simply outdated.

Yes, words do have to come out of your mouth to get clients to buy, but not a lot of words. A good salespreneur knows this:

Salespreneur = Questions **Clients Buying** = Them Talking, Not YOU

A new question allows your clients to see and imagine what their life could be. A sales pitch only allows them to see life from their current framework. It's time to make the shift from selling to questioning: a shift from you selling for your reasons to the client buying for his/her reasons.

e) External Selling vs. Internal Buying

Questions help make the shift from external selling to internal buying. What the heck does that mean?

1) External selling is getting the client to buy for general reasons. You give them reasons why the product is great and how everyone is using it and how it got rated the best product by all the rating services. People may buy because you sold it well, but they won't be fulfilled unless they are doing it for their reasons.

2) Internal buying is when you tap into clients' deepest desires and they come up with their own reasons for buying and their own reasons for how this will fulfill them. The reasons for buying are no longer general but specific and personal. The reason the client now has specific and personal reasons for buying is because you took the time to ask the right QUESTIONS within a process that you know delivers results.

f) Questions = Confidence

What does this have to do with confidence? It's simple: he who asks the questions is in control of the meeting. He who asks the questions just needs to show up and guide the client in the specific direction that your client's answers are leading you. How easy is that? Are you more confident going into a meeting that is easy and produces specific results, or would you like to go back to the Neanderthal way of selling for general reasons and guessing outcomes. I'd rather hit the bull's eye every time, wouldn't you?

Activity:

Take a moment and explain how both you and your customer benefit from Internal Buying.

You?

Your customer?

g) A Good Question is the Start of a Good Process

By now you realize that a good question is the key to making a shift from selling for your reasons to the client buying for his reasons. A good question puts you in charge of the meeting and allows you to be in a state of confidence. A good question is the start of a good process. Questions help us discover more about people and situations. Discovery is what a client meeting and process is all about. So let's talk about processes.

Confidence Builder # 3: Process

"We enjoy the process far more than the proceeds." - Warren Buffet

What is the point of having a process?

Warren Buffet, one of the wealthiest men on the planet enjoys the process of creating his empire even more than he enjoys the proceeds. The end result, the sale in your case, is only a small part of a glorious and magnificent experience resulting from a process. It is in the process that we learn, grow, experience and gain insights that never could have been possible otherwise. A great chef has a process for baking a pie, a super bowl quarterback has a process for throwing the football, an artist has a process for creating a painting and a sales entrepreneur must have a process for creating an incredible client experience. Show me anyone who is consistently successful and I will show you a consistent process behind that success.

Try this process on for size with your client. I call it "the visioning process." For now I will just share the question with you, so you can experience the power of a single question within an incredible process for systematic results, not to mention incredibly happy customers whose lives you will shake and whose world you will rock because they are so damn happy with the new vision for themselves. Here it is:

Imagine for a moment you and I are having this conversation and its three years into the future. We're both sitting on an island sipping some margaritas, and you are now reminiscing about the last three years of your life's journey. As you look back over the last three years, what must have happened for you to say it was the most incredible three years of your entire life?

- Personally?
- Professionally?
- Fun and entertainment?
- Contribution?

And you shut up and let your client talk. A question like this allows for a strategy to be formulated between you and your client. It takes all guessing out of the equation. This is an amazing process that will change your world and your client's world! I will teach you how to execute it later. For now I want to demonstrate the point of having a process.

Many people have told me that the clients they work with won't go through a process such as "The Visioning Process." That is okay; this question can be reframed for any type of meeting. Someone recently told me that the way they sell is by delivering a presentation to a group of people. Here is how I would handle a situation where you have 10-30 minutes to deliver a presentation to this small group or even a large group.

- Engage the audience: Mr. Client/audience, you know that I'm here to talk about "X" today. Before we begin, imagine I just gave you a 30 minute presentation on "X" Product and now you're evaluating what you just heard. What must have happened for you to say it was the best 30 minutes you've spent this week?
- If it was a large audience, they can just write down their responses and they will look at their responses at the end of the presentation and only they will know if you were on point. The point is, you have engaged them and they are paying attention.

- If it was a small group, you can have a few people in the group answer your question and you will know exactly what to weave into your presentation right before you are about to deliver it.
- Now, you have feedback to improve and innovate your presentation moving forward.

The whole point of having questions or processes like these is to engage your customer and inspire their reasons for action. When people come to their own self-realizations, they will take action.

A Process:

- Reduces the sales cycle
- Increases your chances of acquiring a client
- Increases your confidence

a) A Process Reduces the Sales Cycle

Everything in the world is speeding up today as a result of technology. Today, sales people have a quick sales pitch because they want to make money and need to make money. A quick sales process ends up confusing the customer, mixing up information and you end up losing the customer. Even if you don't lose the customer, you spend precious time trying to correct where you screwed up.

Warning: YOUR SALES PROCESS SHOULD NOT SPEED UP. IT IS HAZARDOUS TO BOTH YOU AND YOUR CLIENT'S WELL BEING AND IT WILL COST BOTH OF YOU LOTS OF MONEY.

A confused client = A slow acting client.
It actually costs you money and your reputation.

On the other hand, the more thorough you are, the more you will spot opportunities that you never would have been aware of.

Opportunities = An Excited Client
An Excited Client = A Fast Acting Client
A Fast Acting Client = A Reduced Sales Cycle

All of this is happens because of a thorough and diligent process.

By now you realize, a quick sales pitch is the wrong way to go. By using a process, such as the processes I share in this book, you will learn how to go deep with the customer in a short period of time and you will never again wonder WHY your potential client isn't calling you back. Quite the opposite, they will be beating down the door to speak with you. You will actually reduce the sales cycle and time. You will execute efficiently and effectively when the client is clear and is inspired to take action quickly.

A Process = Clarity and focus for your client **Clarity and Focus** = Speed of implementation and execution

When a client is clear and focused, procrastination doesn't exist. Your client is able to be decisive. Indecision leads to doubt, which leads to fear, which leads to procrastination. A process eliminates all of that and in turn reduces the sales cycle.

b) A Process Increases your Chances of Acquiring Clients

Why does a process increase your chances of acquiring a client? There are several reasons:

- When you are thorough and calculated in your approach, your process becomes simple for your client who is experiencing it for the first time. Simple is better and better means more clients. If you have a step-by-step process and your client is clear on the steps, you will get more clients to buy.
- A good process takes the pressure off you and puts the primary focus on your client. When you have a process you can relax and be confident. Rather than having the focus on yourself and worrying about screwing up, you are now relaxed and focused on one thing—your customer. Remember, an effective process is question driven and is focused on the customer, not on you.
- A process delivers predictable and consistent results. When a process is effective, you know why it works. When you know why something works you can do it over and over again. The results end up being predictable. When you can predict a result, you will be inspired to do it over and over, which will lead to consistent success for you as a salespreneur.

Are you more right brained or left brained?

The left brain is more logical, more sequential, more analytical and more process driven. When I talk about a process and we think of things as a process, we are using our left brain. A process is often linear, follows a particular set of steps and if you follow those steps you can predict a certain result.

The right brain is the more creative part of your brain. Personally, I am more right brained and we will talk about this in the next confidence builder.

c) <u>A Process = Confidence</u>

When you can predict an outcome in advance, do you have more or less confidence going into the situation? That's why a process is a confidence builder.

Have you ever watched a sporting event where the athlete makes almost every shot or completes every pass or scores a goal every time? In the box, you hear the broadcasters or the fans saying, "It's amazing! He is automatic!" At that point, the athlete doesn't have to think anymore or focus on the process because it is automatic for him. He has practiced the shot or taken the shot a million times before and what he does on the field now is miraculous, it is a work of art. You can imagine the confidence he has!

I have a handful of the BEST processes for selling that I share throughout this book. Each one will produce a different result for each stage of the selling process. Each one has certain steps or sequences to follow. Once you master those steps, then you can let loose and let your creative genius come out. Remember, the mastery is in the doing and the practicing. Think, Michael Jordan. Think, work of art!

Activity: What's your morning routine (process) to get you ready for the day?

List the ten things you do in the morning to get ready for your day

You probably didn't realize it until just now, but your morning routine is a process that gets you a specific result. At the end of the process you're awake, clean, dressed, on time, well fed and ready. Imagine if you went to your office without clothes, hungry and smelling terrible. How confident would you be?

For the most basic things we have processes and for the really important things - like selling - we shortcut the process and we settle for mediocre results, don't we? My advice to you is never shortcut the process. You will only be short changing your own confidence and your customers' dreams.

As I mentioned earlier, I share several powerful processes with you throughout this book. Stick with me. You are going to be enjoying a brand new, prosperous career very soon.

Confidence Builder # 4: Intuition- Be Your Best Self

"The creative is the place where no one else has ever been. You have to leave the city of your comfort and go into the wilderness of your intuition. What you'll discover will be wonderful. What you'll discover is yourself." - Alan Alda

Now that you understand the importance of a process, let's talk about Intuition. What is intuition and how do you tap your intuition?

Intuition - An Instinctive Knowing Without Using Rational Processes

Let's talk about how intuition plays a role in your client process. When most people think of a process, their rational mind takes over and looks for the steps in the process. Following certain steps is what will make you partially successful in your client process. However, it's not the entire solution for you to achieve the ultimate result. An actual step by step linear and rational process, coupled with one's intuition, is what creates the ultimate sales process and client experience.

Right Brain = Intuitive Mind (creativity, imagination, holistic view)
Left Brain = Linear or Rational Mind (logical, process oriented, sequential, analytical)

When you are able to access your linear mind (left brain) and intuitive mind (right brain) at the same time, this is called being in your FULL POTENTIAL, or Presence.

A process creates confidence and when you are confident, you are freer to be who you really are. A process allows you to freely access your intuition and makes the experience for the client even more powerful. How? By using a process as your guiding PATH, your intuition becomes your guiding FORCE and will then be freed up to do its thing.

Always use your intuitive mind, it will allow you to imagine with your client, envision, dream and create a bigger future together. If you're just using the steps in the process, then you're stuck in your left brain and you won't be able to relate or connect with your client. If you just use your intuition (right brain), you won't have a road map or compass to guide you when you're off course. The two of them together allow you to be present and presence is where all solutions to life's problems come from. Remember why your client is sitting in front of you: to solve a problem or to capitalize on an opportunity. It's one or the other. Have - and trust - your process, but balance it with intuition.

Napoleon Hill, author of the Book, *Think and Grow Rich* interviewed 500 of the most successful people in the world in order to discover what made them so successful. Napoleon Hill asked, "What made these 500 people so successful? What was the one thing they had in common?" Here is a summary of what all 500 people stated, "Anytime I had a big business decision to make I was able to tap into the intuitive part of my mind to know whether or not it was the right decision for me." Their intuition was always right and that's what made them successful. Knowing what you know now, doesn't it make sense for you to develop your intuition? Modeling successful people is another key to your success.

When you are able to use your intuition you are then able to operate in your full potential as a salespreneur. Right now, you may be asking what does your intuition have to do with sales. It has everything to do with sales and everything to do with your success. All of your most creative, ingenious and best ideas have come because of your intuition. Have you ever amazed yourself with an idea and then said, "How did I come up with that?" It was intuition. Intuition is key to your success and mastery in sales.

"The intuitive mind is a sacred gift and the rational mind is a faithful servant. We have created a society that honors the servant and has forgotten the gift." - Albert Einstein

Are you ready to experience your Full Potential?

Would you like to be Present in your client meetings?

Do you think your results would improve if you were present with your clients?

Does it make sense to access all of your potential in a client meeting?

Do you want me to share a process for you to be in your Full Potential all the time?

I know your answers are YES, YES, YES, YES and YES.

Let me explain. There is a scientific process for you to be in your Full Potential whenever you choose. In your Full Potential, you are CONFIDENT, passionate, inspired, energetic, healthy, etc. Would you like to be in your Full Potential at all times, especially before a client meeting?

Have you ever heard a parent say, "Be your best self in school today" or a coach say to a ten year old athlete, "Be your best today"? Automatically when we hear this as kids or athletes we know what it means. We can imagine it and picture it and we go into that mode of being our best. Somehow as adults we have lost or forgotten how to "Be your best self." It's simple and completely life changing when you can Be Your Best Self on command, especially before or during a client meeting. All your guidance, all your creativity, all your solutions to problems, comes from being your Best Self. We call this your Full Potential Self.

I am not exaggerating when I tell you that this process has completely transformed my relationships, my business and even my destructive habits over the last four years. This process works and I wouldn't share it with you if I didn't know for a fact that this alone will increase your confidence by ten times over.

Make a promise to yourself that you will do the following exercise every morning when you wake up. I DO!!!!!!! (This is a scientific process I am about to share with you. The science is called Holodynamics, founded by my friend and mentor Vernon Woolf.)

Activity:

1) **Go to a Peaceful Place.** In a moment I'm going to have you go to a peaceful place in your mind. Why and what does this have to do with sales? Everything. In a peaceful place, your brain/mind is at rest and you are able to access ideas and solutions that you cannot when your mind is busy. When you are in a peaceful state you can be present and connect with your clients. Do you think your clients want you to be present with them? Do you think your clients want you to come up with creative ideas? Do you think your clients want you to co create ingenious solutions with them? Oh, by the way, do you think this would increase your confidence? Touchdown!!!!!!

Let's do it: Go to a peaceful place in your mind. Examples: A sunset, a place in your house, a favorite place from childhood, the beach – somewhere where you feel safe, that's peaceful and quiet.

Are you there? Good. Now you're ready for step 2.

2) **Be Your Best Self?** While you are in your place of peace, imagine your Best Self (you at your Full Potential) coming towards you. What do you look like, what do you feel? Are you more energized, confident, passionate, inspired, relaxed, and courageous?

Some of you will see an image of you, others will see symbols that represent you, and some of you will see colors that represent you. It's all good. If you don't get an image right away or if you have trouble, practice every day and your image will become clearer and clearer. For some people, their Full Potential has been on holiday for a while. It's not uncommon for some people to just get a feeling instead of an image.)

When you IMAGINE your Best Self coming towards you, you are using your intuitive, creative and imaginative part of your mind. When you are being your Best Self (your Full Potential), you are in both your right brain and your left brain at the same time and this means that you are PRESENT.

Presence or Being Your Best Self is the key to a successful client meeting. Think of how you will be able to connect with your customer, think of the questions you will dream up and the creative solutions you will tap into. Straight up, you will be in the Zone. This will make you a master in the art of sales and influence.

The point I am making here is you now have another confidence builder. Anytime you want, before a client meeting or during a client meeting you can go to your Place of Peace and invite your Best Self to join you. Scientifically speaking, it only takes 1/70th of a second. Now, you can be CONFIDENT any time you want in any situation. Congratulations!

The greatest part about this process is for you to communicate with your Best Self before your client meetings. Ask your Best Self questions and follow the messages, answers and guidance that you receive for each meeting. This is a simple formula to be your best rather than being nervous, anxious or confused before a client meeting.

As your Best Self, you are able to be process oriented and intuition oriented at the same time. That's the formula for success in sales.

Communicating With Your Best Self:

Make it a daily habit to go to your place of peace and invite your Best Self to join you.

- Every day you can communicate with your Best Self
- Ask your Best Self questions
- Write down messages from your Best Self and follow them
- Get used to being your Best Self

Notice the qualities you have as your Best Self and ask yourself, "Would this be useful to me in a sales situation?" That's an easy answer…YES!!!!

Confidence Builder #5: Flexible and Conversational

"The dialogue between client and architect is about as intimate as any conversation you can have, because when you're talking about building a house, you're talking about dreams." - Robert A. M. Stern

"Never doubt that a conversation can change a relationship, indeed it is the one thing that always has." - Ted McGrath

When I was 21 and started in business, I got myself an appointment with the CEO and largest shareholder of *Dixon Ticonderoga Company*. You know the #2 pencils you used on the SAT's? That's right; that's him. Dixon is a multi-hundred million dollar company. I got the meeting with Gino Paolo because it was one of the company's I interviewed with before I signed on with New York Life. I called him and told him I wanted to buy him breakfast so I could learn from his wisdom and success. He said he didn't do breakfasts or lunches but I could meet with him in his office.

Gino didn't make it past the fourth grade but was a brilliant business person. Here is a summary of his wisdom. "Listen kid, pretty soon, you're going to end up driving a Lincoln and your friends are going to be driving Buicks." (I was already driving a Mercedes, so I knew what he was getting at.) "You are going to be hanging around successful business people and your friends are going to be hanging out at crummy bars. You are going to be dressed well and polished and they will still be wearing college clothes. You have to make a decision of what direction you want your life to go. That's up to you. And one more thing; in this world you have to have BIG BALLS, huge ones."

At the end of his speech, I kid you not, I said, "Well since you have to have big balls, huge ones, I'm going to follow your advice." I stood up, walked up to his desk, placed my hands on the desk and said, "I would like to take over your company's 401k plan and let New York Life Investment Company manage it." He was stunned and so was I and so was Tucker, my brother, who was standing there with me. He buzzed in his secretary and told her to give us the plan documents, and that's how it's done. We never got the account because it turned out his bank sits on his board and manages his investment plan. I will tell you what, that was a HUGE account and it took "huge balls" to do what I did. Gino knew that I had them, so he had to give me a shot.

I share this story with you for only one reason. I showed up to Gino's office prepared to do one thing. Have a simple conversation to get him to talk and share his wisdom with me. Do you know how I got him to talk? He said, "Okay Ted, what are you trying to sell me today?" And I said, "Absolutely nothing. I just came here because

I wanted to learn from you Gino. I am starting in a business and I am having amazing success right now and I know you were in my shoes at one time as well. Tell me, how did you get started in your business?" I asked the question, I shut up and I waited to see where the conversation would take me. I had no intention of selling him anything. I guess I got a little carried away.

"Enthusiasm is one of the most powerful engines of success. When you do a thing, do it with all your might. Put your whole soul into it. Stamp it with your own personality. Be active, be energetic, be enthusiastic and faithful and you will accomplish your object. Nothing great was ever achieved without enthusiasm." - Ralph Waldo Emerson

We talked about the importance of having a process earlier and I shared the visioning question with you to show you the power of that process. Oftentimes sales people will blow the process because they don't know how to lead into the process in a conversational manner. They will jump right into it and the client feels like he is being interviewed. Many people don't like to be put on the spot like that. Here's the secret. You start with some "steering questions" to steer your client into the direction of your process and then you take them on the journey of a lifetime, a journey into their ultimate vision for their life. This is exactly what I did with Gino. Before you get to the ultimate journey here are the two questions I would ask to get you there safely.

1) Tell me about your family.
2) How did you get started in your career/business?

People love to talk about their family and their business. Once you get the person talking, the rapport is built and then you have permission to go deeper. When you don't use steering questions such as these, you can go an entire meeting without connecting with the client. And you wonder why sales people don't "get the sale"!!!!!!! These types of questions are critical to create the space for real, authentic and meaningful conversations to arise. I go deeper into this in later chapters.

Someone once told me, "In life most conversations are trivial and inconsequential." To me this means that most conversations have no point to them. Every interaction I have with people, I want it to be rich and filled with meaning.

Too many times in a sales situation, the conversation never scratches the surface of the client's desires and visions. Oftentimes questions are just asked to retrieve information, rather than to retrieve the true essence of the person you are interacting with. A salesprenuer wants the true essence of his client and uses the Power of Conversation to get it.

The Power of Conversation breeds confidence in the client relationship. When you engage in a deep and meaningful conversation with a client, a certain bond and trust is developed, even if you have only known each other for minutes. With a process that stimulates this type of conversation you can be extremely confident that your client will confide in you and trust your recommendations. When a client confides in you, how confident does it make you feel that they are going to buy from you? They don't just buy the product, they buy the experience and your ability to communicate in an authentic manner will determine your success. Why not have a process that supports that?

Activity:

Think back to the last meaningful conversation you had with a friend, a family member or a client. What happened in that conversation that made it powerful? List the reasons that made it powerful.

Flexible and Conversational: Make sure your process (client meeting) isn't an interview but rather a conversation. Be sure to be flexible during your interaction with your clients. Don't be so rigid that you follow the process step by step and you leave no room for conversation or innovation to arise. And don't be so flighty that you allow the client to get off on a tangent in areas that have nothing to do with moving them forward in a focused and specific direction that creates an outcome. If they want to get on a tangent and express themselves, let them do it and use your process and structure to guide them back and refocus them when it's appropriate. Don't be too rigid with the process, but know that you are there to create an outcome that means ACTION. Make it fun and interactive. Enjoy yourself.

Once you become a master in sales and influence, the depth and power of your conversations with customers will make for a truly enriching customer experience. Clients will share their deepest treasures with you and you will cherish every interaction. In light of the processes you will learn in this book, you will be very intentional with each one of your client's desires and you will know exactly how to guide them to achieving the specific outcome they are looking for. There is true power in having a process that promotes questions, conversations and intentional outcomes.

Confidence Builder # 6: Power Habits

"Habit is either the best of servants or the worst of masters." - Nathaniel Emmons

Manage your emotions and you will master your result. All of sales and influence is about being in the right emotional state yourself and inspiring your clients into an emotional state that will get them to take action on buying your product. To consistently be in a confident and resourceful state you must develop a set of Power Habits that automatically put you in that state. I call them Power Habits because it allows you to access the unlimited power that's within you. I break them down into 2 categories:

a) Daily Power Habits: the habits that I use every day to get me in a confident state.

Examples:

- Going to My BEST SELF (as you experienced earlier)
- Reading or listening to an audio program in the morning
- Drinking my wheat grass and taking my vitamins
- Going for my run while listening to audio programs
- Having a morning call with my team to jump start my day
- Reprogramming my mind for success before bed time
- Writing my books

What can you do on a daily basis to get yourself into the right emotional state?

Activity:

Develop Five Daily Power Habits that automatically trigger a strong confident emotional state for you.

1.
2.
3.
4.
5.

Examples: Exercise, rituals, audio programs, prayer/meditation, connecting with inspiring relationships early in the day, etc….

If you don't have any Power Habits currently, it's okay. Create five, but start by implementing at least one Daily Power Habit.

b) Situational Power Habits: habits that I use for certain situations, as necessary.

For example, before each seminar or speaking engagement I program my subconscious mind to deliver the results that I want before I go on stage. It's a five minute ritual. I say to myself, "I command my subconscious mind to deliver inspirational, powerful, life changing results for my audience. I am the voice for change. I am the voice for change." I repeat this over and over again out loud; I get my entire physiology involved as well as the tonality of my voice. Two things happen as a result: a) by the time I get on stage I am 100% ready to deliver and all the information starts flowing through me. It's as if I opened up the floodgates of inspiration. b) I am in a powerful emotional state because I used my body, language and tonality in such a way that I have triggered incredible excitement, confidence and inspiration within me.

Can you imagine doing this for five minutes straight? By the time I am done, my body is vibrating and I am in a peak emotional state to deliver in a powerful and confident manner. When I am in this emotional state, what do you think the likelihood of FEAR entering my space is? ZERO percent chance.

Activity:

1) Stop now and create your own Power Statement to speak out before your next sales meeting or presentation.

Power Statement:

Do you know how I know this works? I have tried meetings doing this ritual beforehand and not doing this ritual, and there is a world of difference.

2) Before your next meeting I want you to say your Power Statement out loud for five minutes straight. Really get your body into it as well as the tonality of your voice.

This is a ritual I do to get into a peak state. Now let me share a more specific and calculated technique. Different strokes for different folks.

What if you could get into this peak emotional state in less than five minutes? I still do this for five minutes before I go on stage because I literally want my body to be erupting with power. However, you can get yourself into a peak state in a matter of seconds. Suppose you are feeling a bit off because you had a bad meeting, a bad phone call, a bad day. You can't always change the situation but you can change the way you feel about it. I want you to take a moment and remember a time where you felt like you could do no wrong; a time where you felt like you were in the zone; a time where you felt incredibly successful; a time where you felt happy. Right now I am going to show you how to anchor that feeling into your body anytime you want.

"Anchoring" is a method of turning an undesirable feeling into a resourceful feeling in a few seconds. Anchoring allows you to change the way you feel about something whenever you want to by creating a stimulus response pattern.

Imagine if you could go from feeling completely nervous in a client meeting to feeling 100 percent confident in a few seconds. Do you think your sales would go up 100 percent?

Anchoring:

The steps of anchoring:

1) Know what emotional state you want to be in. Do you want to be confident, calm, powerful, inspired? Choose the state of how you want to feel. Just choose one. I will help you anchor the state that you just selected.
2) Write down or remember one experience from your past where you felt the desired state you just selected. If you can't remember ever feeling like that, it's ok. Rather than re-live the experience, you can imagine it as if it were happening.
3) Re-live or imagine that experience as if it is happening right now. Use your senses and notice what you were feeling, hearing and seeing.
4) As you re-live the experience allow it to build up to its peak state and then allow it to subside. If you're only feeling it at a level four right now, build it up to where you are feeling it at a level ten. Once you get to your peak (level ten), then let go and release that feeling.
5) Are you ready to start anchoring this peak state within you? Now I want you to repeat the process again and right as your state is about to peak: a) Make a unique gesture with your hand, such as a fist pump. b) Scream a word or sentence out loud, such as "power." c) Create an image in your mind that represents your desired state, such as a powerful image of you. These are called anchors. Do all three of these simultaneously. The secret is to do all three of them at the same time, right before you're about to peak at a level ten.
6) Once you peak, stay in that peak state for a few seconds and then break the state completely by releasing your anchors (the fist, the image and the word you're saying out loud). Releasing the anchors means erase the mental image from your mind, let go of your gesture, and stop saying your word/sentence. You can break the state quickly by changing the image in your mind and changing your physiology.
7) Repeat the entire process of steps 1-6 again six times. Be sure to repeat it six times. It's very important to break your state, before you repeat the process again. If you don't break the peak state, the anchoring process won't work.

How do you know if the anchoring process worked?

You can be sure the anchoring process works by testing it a few times. After you have repeated the process six times, see if the anchor was successful. Make your unique gesture, say your word or words and call upon the image that represents your desired sate. Do all three of them simultaneously and see if you immediately go to your desired state. If nothing happens within ten seconds then you didn't do the process right. You should be able to fire off just one of the anchors and immediately go into state. So, do the anchoring process over again until you get it right.

You can see how powerful this process can be in a client meeting. When you can achieve your desired state on command, you can achieve your desired result. The right state has everything to do with the right results.

Why are Power Habits critical to your business?

The emotions you arrive with are what will be transferred to your clients in your meeting. If you are tired, they will be tired. If you are inspired, they will be inspired.

Emotion creates motion and your end goal is to get you clients into motion because Motion = ACTION.

When you are able to choose exactly how you want to feel in a client meeting, you would probably agree that your feelings are going to determine how you behave and how you react to situations. I believe that many sales people put the pressure on their clients and try to close because they feel like they are losing control of the situation. They get a little resistance from their client and they don't know how to handle it. Instead of embracing the resistance and changing how they feel about it immediately, they resist it and create tension in the client meeting. At the time your client is resisting, doesn't it make sense for you to go into a calm and relaxed emotional state? When you are calm and relaxed you can easily talk through and handle any objections or resistance that comes up.

Imagine for a moment that you can go to a calm and relaxed state when a client objection comes up, which you know you can once you anchor this state.

Activity:

1) If you haven't anchored a calm and relaxed state yet, do it now.
2) Once you anchor going to a calm and relaxed state on command, now let's bring in the exercise from Confidence Builder #4. Imagine your Best Self coming towards you. Once your Best Self is with you, you will easily come up with creative solutions to someone's objections.

Why are you able to come up with creative solutions to their objections? When you are in your Best Self you don't get sucked in to their resistance or you don't get sucked into your own down draft behavior when their resistance comes up. When you are in your Best Self, you won't "close" the person because you are coming from a place of potential solutions rather than problems. You actually won't force solutions on them; you will be a facilitator to help them create their own solutions. You will be a co-creator in the process.

Now that you have anchored in the state and your Best Self is with you, handle the resistance with the proper language. Oops, I'm jumping ahead to the last chapter. We will get to this later.

By now you're starting to see why *Never Be Closing* is incredibly powerful, aren't you?

Confidence Builder # 7: Inspired Action

"Only one thing makes a dream impossible: the fear of failure." - The Alchemist

Inspired Action: Action is the natural byproduct of inspiration. When your clients are inspired, they will take action. When you are inspired, you take action. Most people want to motivate others through external forces that bring about pain or pleasure. And these techniques do work, but it's much more powerful to truly figure out what inspires your clients and then help them run hard to meet their objectives. It's easier to run swiftly with the internal force of inspiration guiding you than to run up against a brick wall. Despite what people think, it's easier to inspire someone, rather than close them in the conventional sense of "closing." Let's explore.

How do you inspire your client?

Simple. You don't just sell your product, you sell your passion. People buy your passion first and the product second. Howard Schultz doesn't just sell coffee. In fact in interviews, he rarely mentions the coffee. He sells the experience Starbucks offers. He sells, "the third place between work and home where people can feel comfortable gathering." For Steve Jobs, it isn't just about the hardware he sells, such as the iPod. He's passionate about how he can enrich people's lives by giving them access to their favorite music. He's passionate about, "making a dent in the universe." He is a salespreneur. A salespreneur must have a messianic zeal about making the world a better place. You can easily be financially successful in a sales job you hate; people do it all the time. But unless you have passion, you will never inspire people. People want to be inspired today, and yes they want to be inspired by you.

What is sales and influence really about? Here is one of the answers: to inspire someone into future action, you must know what already inspires them.

Up until this point you have heard me reinforce this revolution in thought of *never be closing*. After all, it is the name of this book and I want you to fully embrace this mentality and the way of the salespreneur.

Let me introduce a simple tool to inspire action in your life and in your clients. Most of the time at the end of a meeting, people write down what they are going to do or what they're going to change in their life and then they never do it. You see this after a two day seminar or a simple meeting. You see this with your clients. Let's start with you. Here I want to demonstrate the power of inspiration vs. closing. This requires us to go deeper than we are used to going, with ourselves as well as our clients.

The Inspired Action Sales Tool:

What has inspired you so far in this book? List three things:

1)

2)

3)

To inspire others you need to be inspired. List five things that inspire you:

1) What song inspires you?

2) How much money inspires you?

3) What vacation inspires you?

4) What relationship inspires you?

5) What person inspires you?

6) What else inspires you?

When you tap your inspiration, you tap something even deeper than WHY you are doing an action. WHY you are doing something is a powerful reason to follow through. But what inspires you will ignite the passion behind your reasons why. Imagine being inspired! Now couple that with a strong enough reason why. I could have a strong reason to meet my sales quotas because if I don't, I'm going to be the worst person in the office this month and I will be embarrassed. That's a strong reason why, wouldn't you agree? What's it missing? Even if you meet your quotas to save embarrassment, you could still feel crappy about yourself and that's not inspiring. That may only save you for one more month and next month you end up quitting.

Think about how this applies to your clients. If you are selling them or "closing" them on a product like insurance because you have them focused on the pain of possibly dying, that is a strong enough reason why. Yet several months down the road, they may have buyer's remorse and drop the coverage or even go work with someone else because they had a terrible experience with you. Sure you "closed the sale," but you lost a client months later.

> *To inspire* is to grow with your client.
> *To "close"* is to shrink with your client.
> *Life* is growing.
> *Death* is shrinking.

Let's examine the power of inspiration and the process that ignites it.

Inspire: I was inspired after my seminar the other day because I felt totally connected to my audience. Notice that the inspiration isn't just coming from the seminar; it's coming from the connection with my audience. The connection is a feeling I'm having.

If you are my coach or a salespreneur wanting me to take action, you will want to use words like "connection" because you know that language inspires me to take action.

I could easily think about the situation from the reverse perspective. I could say to myself, "I have to motivate myself to get the sale today because I have to pay all the employees in my company." Is that completely different than what inspires you about a situation? If you are just focused on motivating reasons then you may spend your whole life in a state of worry and that state of worry triggers you to go perform. Sure, you may get results, but your whole life is spent worrying. Do you see my point?

You may get your clients to buy and they may just be motivated to buy because they are worried. Do you want to be a worried sales person, with worried clients, or do you want to be an inspired salespreneur? The choice is yours. This is your defining moment.

Inspired Reason: (WHY) - Why did that inspire me? Notice how we're taking it a layer deeper here.

I am inspired when I connect with my audience because I know that will inspire them to take action, and my clients and I will both get the results we're looking for. My reason why is not just to feel connected, it's to get a result for my client and for me. Do you see how this works?

Inspired Action: What three actions will you take as a result?

- I will instantly set up my next seminar.
- I will increase my goals of having a larger audience.
- I will record my seminars so more people can get access to me.

Notice where these actions come from. They come from the core of my inspiration, which is to CONNECT. I love to CONNECT. Without focusing in on what INSPIRES me, it is easy for me to leave a seminar and not follow through. If I just did the seminar and didn't go through this exercise of what inspired me, I may have just left and done nothing. It's quite possible that I could have been content with my results and just moved on to something else that needed my attention. It's just as easy for your clients to end a meeting with you and do nothing, if they aren't inspired.

However, this is about what inspires you and when you are focused on inspiration, you come from a powerful place where you can create anything you want. When you are inspired, you don't see the obstacles you normally see because you feel different. This is simple, yet powerful insight.

Activity:

Inspiration: For your next client meeting ask your client, "What inspired you about our meeting today?" For example, what inspired you about the house you just saw, or what inspired you about the car you just drove?

Inspired Reason: Why did that inspire you, Mr. Client?

This is a very important question. If you are selling someone a car, and they just test drove that car, and you are now asking them what inspired them and why it inspired them, when they come back the next day, you can bring up the words they used so they instantly remember why they want to have your product or service. Remember, it's not your words that get them to buy, it's *their* words.

Right now you might be thinking, "I feel weird asking someone what inspires them." Well, once you start feeling inspired yourself, you will want to inspire everyone else, and then you will "never be closing" again because you will be asking different questions that evoke different emotions.

Inspired Action: What actions would you like to take as a result of this? Or, what are the next steps for you, Mr. Client? (Don't worry if he is not sure, because you know what inspires him and you know your process, so just tell him what the next action steps are.)

The beauty of this process is that you are tapping into your clients' emotion and people buy on emotion. Next, you are finding out their reason for being inspired and that also helps your clients tap into their logical mind of why they want to buy. Then you are having them tell you what actions they want to take ownership of.

I believe you are now getting a strong sense that when someone is inspired in a client meeting, you don't have to use outdated closing techniques that people don't appreciate and that make others uncomfortable.

We have only skimmed the surface of Inspired Action. I gave you general questions to determine what inspires people. What I just shared with you is only the foundation of what you will learn in upcoming sections. I will teach you to master this method of Inspired Action through a life changing process called "The Five Fundamental and Fulfillment Needs." This is one of the most powerful forces in life and business for inspiring others into action.

When you and your clients are taking MASSIVE action in your life, and the results are pouring in, what do you think this will do for your confidence? As Tom Cruise shouts in the movie "Jerry Maguire", "SHOW ME THE MONEY!"

Activity:

Questions to unleash your inspiration:

1) What can you be the best at?

2) What are you most passionate about?

3) What drives your financial engine?

Activity:

Out of the Confidence Builders in this chapter, what are the top two you feel you need to focus on immediately?

1)

2)

"The inches we need are everywhere around us, they are in every step of the game, every minute, every second. Look at the guy next to you. Look into his eyes; I think you are going to see a guy who is willing to go that inch with you. Because when it all comes down, that's gonna be the fucking difference between winning and losing, between living and dying." - Al Pacino's famous speech to his football team in the movie, "Any Given Sunday"

Don't worry I'm not going to quote athletes through the entire book. I'm not even a huge sports fan, but I did play college athletics and I know how important confidence is in one's life. It's the inches between winning and losing, between living and dying. The inches of extra effort that you put in with the above processes will be the difference between being the BEST and just being great. Your clients will be able to look into your eyes and see whether you have the confidence and whether you are willing to go the extra inch for them. I know you want to be the best, so PLEASE do all the exercises I have prepared for you. I am a guy who is willing to go that inch with you! I will not get off the treadmill; I will go that extra inch. Who's coming with me?

Review of Chapter 1

In the last chapter, we discussed confidence builders for having unwavering confidence in a client meeting. Since we're on the topic of results, let's talk about getting 90% of your results before you show up to the client meeting.

Chapter 2

Getting 90% of Your Results Before You Show Up

How do you get 90% of your result before you show up to a meeting?

In this section, you will learn about the Power of Preparation before showing up to a client meeting. I share with you actual preparation exercises to do before each meeting. These exercise will soon become a habit and you will automatically prepare for every meeting with laser focus. This preparation and focus will help you get results before you even meet with the client. How is this possible? You will soon find out.

Let's talk about The Power of Preparation:

Objectives of this Chapter:
1) Preparing yourself for your client meeting
2) Know what your clients are thinking in advance
3) The 11 Preparation Habits

We mentioned a lot about do, do, do, do, do in the last chapter. Your clients have their "do's" too. Before you go into any presentation or client meeting, it is essential to ask yourself this question: What is my client thinking? Well, if you don't know, here it is:

1) Do I trust this person?

Fundamentally, no one will buy from you unless they like you and trust you. Building rapport is a critical part of a client relationship. To get someone to trust you, you must understand and appreciate his world. When he feels that you understand him and that he is like you, he will trust you. We talk more about building rapport extensively in chapter 5.

2) Do I really need this NOW?

Your job is to get them to WANT it. Let's face it. We live in a "satisfaction now" world. We want the benefits now and if we can't get it or don't need it now, very few of us will buy. Part of the role of a sales entrepreneur is to elicit the desires of their client and have them realize that they really WANT this product and when they buy it they will realize they can't live without it.

Pareto had his 80/20 rule in Confidence Builder # 10. Now let me share with you the McGrath 90-10 Rule: Listen 90%, Talk 10%. During your next client meeting use the McGrath 90-10 rule. This rule is how you get the client to like you and to want what you are offering.

Your talking 10% will get you a 100% result. The trick is to make your communication extremely effective in very few words. This way you talk 10% of the time with 100% impact and your client talks 90% of the time. 90% of the meeting you are listening for your client's needs and desires and how they fit into the process I am about to share with you.

What do all sales people really want going into a meeting? Answer: Freedom of Mind—where you can show up and you don't have to think. You can just be there in the flow and deliver a masterpiece of a meeting. That's the ultimate freedom. An athlete who has the game of his life, just shows up because he is prepared and he lets the game take over. You need to let the process take over. You get one chance. Make it count.

Activity:

Think of your last sales presentation or interaction:

1) What did you do well?

2) What percentage of the time did you talk vs. the time your client spoke?

3) What's one thing that you must improve in your sales presentation or communication with others?

Let's talk about your 10% that will deliver 100% impact. Have you ever walked into a meeting and felt nervous because you had no idea what you were going to say? And when you figured out something to say, there was no order to your thought process? Here's the exact process that will prepare you and your subconscious before the meeting, so when you show up you are on target. I call these the "11 Preparation Habits".

Each of the 11 Preparation Habits starts with a question about your next client meeting.

Preparation Habit #1: What do you already KNOW about your Client?

"You have to start knowing yourself so well that you begin to know other people. A piece of us is in every person we can ever meet." - John MacDonald

It's essential before you go into a client meeting that you already KNOW something about the person you are meeting. This builds the rapport and the connection before you even show up to the meeting. For example, what do I already know about you? Although we have never met, I know something about you. I have prepared for my interaction with you today. I know that:

1) you are a sales entrepreneur
2) you are already successful
3) you are passionate about growth and learning

(Note: This is the formula that I will follow throughout the Preparation Habits. I will pose the question and then share with you three answers. You will notice in the answers and examples that follow that I am answering this exactly how I would prepare for a presentation or a meeting. Not only will you learn how I do it, but you will understand this exercise as it relates to you, the "sales entrepreneur."

a) <u>You are a sales entrepreneur.</u>

All the writing and exercises in this book are directed towards the sales entrepreneur who wants to take his career/business to the next level. Instantly I am able to connect with you as I speak because I am you. I have been down similar roads and have faced similar challenges. My whole way of being and communicating stems from my understanding of what you go through on a daily basis. Since I am like you, you are more likely to trust me. In fact right now you are probably connecting with me on a deeper level.

b) <u>I also know that you are already successful.</u>

I don't mean that you are meeting your monetary goals per se, though you could be. What I mean is that you have the mindset for success. You know that investing in your future and betting on yourself is how you are going to be the Michael Jordan of sales and I appreciate you allocating your time and money towards this. I know you could be out in front of a client making money now and that's why I have spent the time to give you amazing content that is going to help you become a top sales entrepreneur and make 10 times the money.

c) One more thing, you are passionate about growth and learning.

The fact that you have taken the time to learn this material and master it means you are passionate about growth. No one forced you to buy this book. You did it because you value growth, and you and I have that in common.

Before we go into the next ten examples, I want you to really recognize the power of the exercise we just did. It is very simple, yet it takes the client meeting to an entirely new level. Your level of awareness/consciousness is very awake to whom you will be meeting, who you are being in the meeting, and the information you are going to deliver. I'm incredibly excited for you to have this tool. This alone will transform your client meetings, won't it?

Activity:

Your Next Client Meeting

What are three things you already know about your client?

1)

2)

3)

If you know the person you can be specific, if you don't know him, be general. Either way, warm your mind to the person you are about to connect with so he feels special and connected to you.

Everyday business people do research. Not just about their competitors but about their clients as well. Information is still a competitive advantage when it comes to knowing your clients.

Preparation Habit #2: What Must They Know?

Remember in being consistent with the McGrath 90-10 Rule, you only have the floor for 10% of the conversation. So whatever you want the clients to know, condense it into three points and make sure those points are rock solid and have maximum impact.

For example right now as I write to you there are three things you must know: 1) you're going to make a lot of money with me; 2) you are going to know exactly why your clients buy; and 3) the quality of your conversation with clients will determine the quality of your business/life.

a) You're going to make lots of money with me.

I helped brand new sales people in a brand new industry to earn $40,000 their first month. Right before I left New York Life, I helped four people make this money in their first month. I know that whether you are new in sales or new to an industry or if you are 15 years in the industry, these tools will make you big money.

Activity:

What are your money goals this year as a sales entrepreneur? Break it down into parts.

1st Quarter -
2nd Quarter -
3rd Quarter -
4th Quarter -

Why is that important to you?

What's important about money to you?

b) You will learn in depth processes for understanding why clients buy.

Most people never take the time to understand human behavior. When I share with you a quick and simple process for understanding the driving force behind why people buy and make all decisions, how quickly do you think your results will go up? I have never seen a sales course that goes this deep and in today's world, you must go deep with the customer to get them to buy. All products are commoditized today, and you better deliver an amazing experience to inspire clients to buy. Make the experience personal by understanding your client and you will have a relationship for life.

What kind of experience do you want to create for your clients? When you go to the Ritz Carlton the experience is about, "Ladies and gentleman serving ladies and gentleman." That's why people go there and that's why people pay $500 per night for a room.

When someone takes a workshop with me our customer experience is "be your best self now." Not only will you be your "best salespreneur now" at the end of my workshops, my customers will be their best self. We are teaching processes that change their lives. This differentiates us from your regular sales trainer.

c) <u>The quality of the conversation determines the quality of the relationship.</u>

In my 11 years of experience working with thousands of people, I found one thing to be timeless: the quality of your conversation determines the quality of the relationship, and the quality of our relationships determine the quality of our lives. You must have a process with clients that creates a conversation and relationship that is priceless. You must position yourself as the resource to help your client achieve whatever he desires. When you enter that type of conversation through the processes in this book, you aren't a sales person; you are facilitator of your clients' wants and desires. If you want to be highly respected and regarded in your field and as a person, strap in and follow me along for the ride.

Activity:

1) Make a list of the products you sell.
2) Make a list of your top five clients.
3) Write down all the great things those five clients have said about you.
4) Why do you think those five clients have bought from you?
5) Was it the product or was it the experience? The experience, ladies and gentleman is you, not just the product. Sure people like the beds at the Ritz Carlton, but it's the experience that is created there by the people that makes it irresistible.

How can you integrate into your client experience, those great things that your clients say about you? That's what you should be selling!

Activity:

What Must Your Clients Know?

1)

2)

3)

Preparation Habit #3: How do you want them to feel?

"I've learned that people will forget what you said, people will forget what you did, but people will never forget how you made them feel." - Maya Angelou

As you prepare for how you want your clients to feel, remember that people buy on emotion. You better get them to FEEL compelled to buy. You decide what emotion. Remember:

Emotion = Motion
Motion = Action
Action = Buying for the salespreneur.

a) Inspired

Have you ever asked yourself the question: Who am I? When I ask myself this question, one word pops up: INSPIRING. I am an inspirer and I want you to read this book and be inspired. That's how I want you to feel. That's why in this book I don't just give you simple techniques, I also share stories and quotes that will inspire you.

Who are you? Ask yourself this question ten times and write down ten different answers. Notice what keeps coming up for you. When you know yourself you will start to know your customer.

b) Deserved or worthy of making BIG money.

What income would you write down for yourself if you knew you couldn't fail? Write it down now. I know you deserve to make all the money you ever dreamed of. So, dream without restrictions and write down how much money you want to make this year if you knew failure was impossible. This takes the last exercise you did about money and stretches your possibilities. Learn to stretch yourself. Always hold yourself to a higher standard. Now do the exercise again with a different set of thinking.

Many people don't feel worthy of making a lot of money. As a sales entrepreneur I HOPE you believe that you will make big bucks. The secret is to dream without limits as you practice my techniques and processes. Here is WHY: you are going to change peoples' lives with the processes in this book and when you change someone's life, you deserve to make all the money you believe you deserve.

Activity:

If money has been a consistent struggle for you, now is the time to become aware of what beliefs are unconsciously controlling your life. Awareness is the first step to transformation.

1) What are your beliefs about money?

2) What did your parents believe about money?

c) Empowered to take action.

After you receive each tool and process, I want you to feel empowered to take action because I also provide you with tangible tools that allow you to start using them right away. I have a bias towards action and I share these tools with you so you are empowered to make a difference in someone's life. Rock on!

Activity:

1) What are two things that you have been putting off that you must take action on today?

2) Give yourself 24 hours to complete those two actions. All I want you to focus on is those two actions. On day two I want you to focus on four actions that you want to take. As you narrow your focus in this way you will start to accomplish what's most important to you.

Activity:

How do you want your next client to feel?

1)

2)

3)

Preparation Habit #4: What do you want them to imagine?

You see things; and you say, 'Why?' But I dream things that never were; and I say, 'Why not?'

- George Bernard Shaw

Einstein said, "Imagination is more powerful than knowledge." What does this mean in the sales process? It means you can share all the information and knowledge with your clients you want, but if you don't get them to imagine a bigger future and to imagine enjoying the benefits of your product, then nothing happens.

h) Making millions of dollars.

Imagine right now that you are making millions of dollars as a result of this book. How has your life changed? DO IT NOW.

I want you to imagine this bigger future because I want you to see vividly what your life looks like when you are even more prosperous, more confident and more fulfilled. This will give you a strong reason to implement ALL the processes in this book. By seeing a bigger future, you start to take ownership of what is possible in your life. Greater Ownership = Greater Action.

Activity:

What's important about money to you? (Also a great question to ask clients.) List three things now.

1)

2)

3)

b) Your clients thinking you are a dream maker.

I understand that most sales people are somewhat driven by feeling important and significant. Let's face it. We like the awards. We like the big paycheck. Sure, there are other reasons why we do what we do, but I believe we all like the attention and acclamation. Otherwise we could get a desk job and feel safe for the rest of our lives.

It's also very important for our clients to respect us and think highly of us. This is part of feeling fulfilled in our work and that we are making a contribution. I believe this is a driving force for all of us. In fact, I know that being respected/important is - and you will know this for sure in the next chapter.

Imagine what it feels like when your clients see you as a dream maker. What will that feel like going to the office every day? Imagine it now.

Completing these exercises is very important to your success. Don't move on without taking the time to complete all the exercises. Are you committed to being your best self? I know you are, so take the time and put in the effort.

c) Being Passionate with Passionate Relationships

I know that the money is great and the awards are great, but in the long term none of it matters if we don't feel passionate about our work. Imagine how passionate you will be when you master influencing others to follow their passions and their desires.

If you have ever seen the movie "Braveheart," you remember the passion that the character William Wallace (Mel Gibson) had. His passion was ignited by one relationship: the love of his life. That passion moved the hearts and souls of his countrymen to risk everything for one chance at freedom. They fought and won their freedom. Never doubt the impact you can have on one person in your life.

When I talk about passion in my seminars, some people have said, "Passion is such a strong word," as if they hadn't experienced it for years. I am passionate just writing to you right now. I couldn't imagine a life without passion. A life without passion is a life without oxygen. In your career, passion is your lifeline for inspiring people to take action. If you don't have passion, people will feel it. They won't buy and they won't refer you to their friends. Ignite your passion now! IGNITE IT!

Activity:

If you don't know what your passion is, write down five things you love to do. Do it now!

1)
2)
3)
4)
5)

Still having trouble identifying your passion? Remember an experience in your life where you were compelled by a passion to serve and contribute to others.

1) What was that experience?

2) When was that experience?

Your passion is right in front of you. It's who you are.

Activity:

What do you want your next client to imagine?

1)

2)

3)

Notice that when you do your homework before the client meeting, the things you want clients to imagine will start coming out in your dialogue as you explain your product or service. It's quite magical. So don't try and script everything. Allow your imagination and intuition to take over. But know your framework. Your role is to get your client to imagine a bigger future. I had you imagine being more passionate and making millions of dollars. Does this change your excitement for reading this book and becoming a master in sales? Absolutely.

When you get your clients to imagine a bigger future, you will never have to close them. They will be so inspired they will jump out of their chair and take action. That's why this book is called "Never Be Closing."

Preparation Habit #5: What will it cost them if they don't act now?

"The price of inaction is far greater than the cost of making a mistake." - Meister Eckhart

a) Confidence

I want people to know that when you take my course, you will have the confidence you must have when you are in a client meeting. When I am giving a presentation I let my audience know that if they don't take action today, they passed up a chance to be the most confident person on the planet. My methods aren't just teaching sales but they are also teaching how to inspire and influence anyone in your life. When you know these techniques, there's nothing you can't accomplish.

What would be the result in your life if you had ten times more confidence?

b) Years of greatness replaced with mediocrity.

Nobody wants to be mediocre, but if you don't have a coach or a mentor to learn from, you will be. Every second someone waits to buy my products is another second of just being average. If they don't buy mine, then they must buy one that suits them better.

Here's what I know for a fact. I am where I am today because I had an amazing mentor. From the time I was 21 years old, between the hours of 8 a.m. to 9 p.m. at night, I was sitting in front of clients and my sales force, teaching them or taking them through these processes.

You remember the 10,000 Hour Rule we discussed earlier. Three to four hours per day for 10 years = 10,000 hours. I put in three times that amount over the last decade, which means I am a triple expert at these processes. If you haven't read the book "Outliers" by Malcolm Gladwell, check it out. This is how Bill Gates and The Beatles became masters in their field. I'm great at what I do because I learned from the best and put in more than my 10,000 hours over the last 11 years. Mediocre people ponder success while great people take action.

Activity:

What can you be the best at? Write it down now.

In the book "Good to Great" by Jim Collins, he talks about what separates good companies from great companies. Companies like General Electric made a fundamental decision. They said, "If were can't be #1 or #2 in our industry than we will sell the farm." Meaning if we're not the best then we sell that company. Make that decision for yourself. Are you ready be the best?

c) Millions of dollars

My fraternity brother in college, who was four years older than I, walked into my office one day. He sold clothes for a living and when he came to work with me, he made $100,000 off one client his sixth month in the business. I know that when someone has an ongoing relationship with me and my products, he will make BIG dollars and if they pass it up, it will cost him millions of dollars.

Activity:

What will it cost your next client if they don't' act NOW.

1)

2)

3)

"In some of my deepest moments of despair and fear, I have found my greatest inspiration. This is how I know that God is watching."-Ted McGrath

You want your client to take some action after the meeting, correct? Even if it isn't the act of buying right there, it is a step on the path that leads to buying. During your meeting, if you already know the costs to the client before you show up and then you get a unique understanding of his situation in the meeting, you will be able to get enough leverage to help him act.

When I talk about leverage here, this is a good thing. Most people don't take action because they won't give themselves permission to have the things they want. They won't act because of low self esteem or fear they won't make their investment back. You must show your clients that the COST of waiting or not changing is much greater than acting, and that will get them to act. Unfortunately or fortunately, pain and fear are great motivators for people. Many times, it's as simple as you pointing out the obvious of what they already know: it will cost them in the long run if they don't take action on what they want.

However, I want to be clear here. Your role is to inspire your clients to imagine and act on a bigger future. But, when it comes to making the final decision, even in the light of a bigger and better future, some people get paralyzed by fear. Use fear as a motivator, if the inspiration isn't able to pull your clients into action. To do this effectively, you must build rapport and ask the right questions to understand your clients' world. We will share more how to do this in later sections.

I want to be clear: You are not closing your client or pushing him to take action. You *are* simply pointing out that inaction does have its costs in life. This is a fundamental truth. Let me bring this home with an inspiring quote.

"We don't realize the most significant moments of our lives while they're happening. We say to ourselves, there will be other days. We forget that that was the only day." - Movie, Field of Dreams, Moonlight Graham

Preparation Habit # 6: What will they gain if they act now?

One of the ways that people make real change in their lives is through leverage. By leverage, I mean how the belief that we will GAIN something powerful can cause us to take massive action. After all, you want your clients to take massive action based on the notion that they will GAIN something in working with you.

People often wonder how someone can be one person one day and the next day, he has completely transformed his live. Here is the secret. Change doesn't take time. Change happens in a moment. It's the years leading up to that change that take time.

Recently I brought on a new COO with our company. He is an amazing person with such a pure heart. Unfortunately both of his parents just passed away in their late 60's. Now I want you to see how this chain of events transformed Scott's life in a positive way.

Scott used to be overweight. Before his mother passed away, one of her wishes was that he loses weight. Guess what? Scott lost 70 pounds in the last year. Why did Scott suddenly lose the weight now when he had been struggling with his weight for years and had tried every diet method known to man? Because he lost the weight to GAIN something else.

When Scott shared his Mom's final words to him days before she died, I instantly knew what inspired Scott to lose weight and GAIN an enormous freedom. His mom's words were, "Honey, lose the weight for me." When his mom made that request, she got leverage on him. One of Scott's driving needs in life is love/connection/relationship. In Scott's mind, losing the weight meant honoring and loving his mother.

I understand human behavior and what causes people to change, so when I shared my analysis with Scott he had a total breakthrough in his understanding of WHY we do what we do as human beings.

What would Scott gain when he took action?

a) Love from his mother for eternity (in his mind)
b) The opportunity to be healthy and live a long life
c) Connection with his Mom every time he eats healthy

On the flip side, what would it cost him if he didn't lose the wait?

a) His mom's approval
b) Her love in his mind (not in actuality)
c) It would cost him his health.

You're thinking now, what the heck does Scott have to do with a client meeting? It's simple. All people and clients have a leverage point. For some, the leverage isn't what THEY will gain or what it will cost THEM, but how it will impact OTHERS they care about such as their family, wife or co-workers.

In your next sales meeting, look for what your client truly values the most. Many times that is his point of leverage. If he lost that or gained more in that area, do you think it would inspire him/her to make a change?

Again, please notice you aren't closing your client on anything here. You aren't using fear tactics to get him to change. You are simply drawing attention to what's real. When you show someone what's real and it becomes real for him, he will be inspired to make real decisions for real change in his life.

In the next chapter I share how an insight that I revealed to Scott transformed his entire family relationship. Stay tuned!

I want to make one more point to drive this home because it's very important. Everyday people act and make changes in their life because of what they gain or what it will cost them. You need to remember; your clients don't want your product as much as they want the benefits (GAIN) it will provide to them.

There's another riveting scene in "Braveheart" where William Wallace (Mel Gibson) was on his horse addressing his countrymen before they go into battle with the English. His countrymen wanted their freedom and this is what they would GAIN from winning the war. They didn't want to fight the battle, but they did want the ultimate benefit which would be freedom. Why were they afraid to fight and win their freedom? The reason is because they were fearful to take action and risk their lives. Just like your clients are fearful to take action and risk something in their lives, whether it is money or approval or whatever.

Look at the speech that got them to act in the face of fear that got them to act because of what they would GAIN.

William Wallace: What will you do without freedom? Will you fight?

Countrymen: No, we will run and we will live

William Wallace: "Run and you will live, for at least a while. But dying in your beds many years from now, would you be willing to trade all the days from this day to that, for one chance - just one chance - for you to go in there and tell them that they may take our lives but they will never take our FREEEEEEEDDDDDDDOOOOOMMMMM!!!" (And the entire crowd goes nuts and is ready to fight.)

What happened there? William Wallace got leverage on his countrymen and he got them to act. He had them IMAGINE lying in their beds many years from now, dying (cost/pain). Then he had them imagine having their freedom (gain). And that inspired them into action. That's exactly how your client meetings should go, except without the horses and the killing.

They will gain freedom when they act, won't they? They will lose it if they don't. William Wallace got the leverage on them to act. They won their freedom. Help your clients win theirs.

Activity:

What will your next client gain when he acts?

1)

2)

3)

Preparation Habit #7: What objections must you diffuse?

We will talk more about handling objections in upcoming chapters. Just remember; you never *overcome* an objection. The moment you resist your clients or resist anything, the force gets stronger and will eventually defeat you. You don't resist, you *diffuse*. When you diffuse an objection, you welcome it and accept it. The objection becomes your friend and it makes you even more powerful and positioned to get the client to buy.

What Objections Must You Diffuse?

a) Time

You may be thinking you don't have the time to go through this entire book, for example. And I would ask you to consider why you are reading this book right now (or why you are listening to this audio program). If you are serious about growing and taking your career to the next level, then I know that *Never Be Closing* is a skill set that you truly value. Now, when you truly value something and its high on your importance scale, is time ever an issue?

I remember when I was 22 years old and my partner wanted to take me to a three-day meeting with his peer group. One of the things that popped into my mind was that I don't have the time; I would rather be selling. But when I got there, everyone in the room was making seven figures, and I remember that meeting as one of the most important meetings to shape my vision of the future. And I was worried about my time. How foolish!

So you DEFINITELY want to take the time and really read this entire book. IMAGINE the results you will achieve in the future.

Activity:

Opportunity Analyzer

List your top five opportunities right now. Rank each of them on a scale of 1-5.

5 = Immediate action - requires immediate attention and action.

3-4 = Timely action - action within a reasonable time frame.

1-2 = Possible action - maybe someday in the future.

1)

2)

3)

4)

5)

Now you have a system to analyze your opportunities and decide how to spend your time most effectively. This will prevent you from reacting to opportunities and you will be able to proactively make the best decisions with your time. Does this make sense? When you know what's most important to you, you will realize that "I don't have time" is an excuse, not a valid reason. And you will be able to bring this perspective into your client meetings.

b) Money

I want you to think of the last time you had your back up against the wall and you had to figure out a way to get money to solve your problem. Was it your rent or mortgage payment? Was it someone you owed money to? Was it a vacation you really wanted to take? What was it? The bottom line is that when we want something badly enough or when we need to make something happen, we find incredible ways to become resourceful.

I spoke previously about one of my standard sayings, "STEP INTO IT." In fact, all my course participants know me for this saying. What they learn is that anytime you have a great need and you Step into the Situation, you find the resources to make it happen.

Your clients literally have to take a step of faith and STEP into IT. To do that, they have to have a strong reason why they want to buy your product. It's your job to help them get clear on their strong reason for buying. When someone has a strong enough reason for something, is money really an issue? Not really. They can always find a way.

I have a guy who is taking one of my courses called the "Ultimate Prosperity Blueprint." He called me to enroll and told me he was inspired to become a coach and truly help others make breakthroughs in their lives. But first, he wanted to make a breakthrough in his own life.

He called me a few weeks later and here is the transcribed message from my voicemail.

"Hello Ted! This is (ABC). Hey, I just wanted to call and tell you that you are doing it brother! You are making a difference in the world and you are doing it one life at a time. And let you know that the life happens to be mine. And I just would like to thank you and encourage you as I know that sometimes we get caught up in the things of the world and all the stuff that's just happening. But I wanted to call and encourage you brother, that you are doing it and its working. All right? Thank you for being you."

Now, you're probably thinking, "Well Ted, that's a nice story, but so what?" The part you don't know is this man was on unemployment when he first called and had been addicted to drugs years ago.

Now, how can someone on unemployment afford to pay for a course in personal growth? He told me his reason "WHY": he wants to be a coach and inspire other people. He knows what it's like to be down and out, jobless, on drugs and scratching and clawing to recover one's life. He really wanted to make a breakthrough in his life, and he found the way to get the money for one of my courses.

Figure out your client's why and there are no objections. (Later I will share processes on how to figure out your client's "WHY." There's an entire chapter devoted to it.)

c) You're not going to sell me.

I figured I would share a fun objection. We all know people at a workshop or people in a client meeting who are thinking or saying, "You're not going to sell me." As if I have some Jedi mind tricks to use to get them to buy! Here is how I handle this.

Let me set the stage for you. At this point in the client meeting or workshop, I will have developed some rapport with this person. In a workshop, I have the floor and I'm on stage. Everyone knows I'm the expert. I have the energy of the audience on my side and 95% of the audience is with me. But there's always that 5%. When he brings up his objection in front of others, all I have to do is solicit the facts from him. Watch how it's done:

I say, "You're right. I'm not going to sell you. You're the only one who can sell you."

1) Notice that I don't resist him. I embrace him and agree that I'm not going to sell him.
2) I shift the control to him because this is what he wants. I let him know that he is the only one who has the power to make the decision about what he wants.
3) Notice how I understand his world and sincerely let him know that I want to help. I'm telling him, "I understand how you're feeling and I would really just like to learn about your situation to see if I can help out. Even if you don't buy my products, I'm still here to help."
4) I ask questions to learn about his situation as well. I ask, "Can you share with me a bit about your business/career?

Do you have kids? Is this your wife here with you? What does she do?"

5) Pay attention to the series of questions I begin to ask this man to uncover who he is and what he wants. What I am doing here is eliciting information. The more information I have means that I don't have to sell him anything. I just need to feed back to him in the sequence that he feeds it to me, what his life situation is.

So he tells me that:

- His sales are doing well (not outstanding, well);
- His kids are 10, 14 (college is approaching and not paid for);
- His wife, who is at the workshop, works and takes care of the kids.

How could this guy not want to make a change?

That's when I give it to him. I feed back his life exactly how he told me: "Of course I am not going to sell you. You're the only one who can sell you. You are the one who will continue making the income you are making and if your satisfied with 'doing well' that's great. You're the one who has to make the decisions on saving for Jimmy and Sally's education and if you want to continue down your current path, it's your choice. You and your wife are in charge of deciding whether she will continue to work full time or if she will take a break from working outside the home so she can focus on the kids' future. I'm sure that you are happy and life will work out for you.

"Let me take a moment and say this to you from the bottom of my heart: If you would like your business and your life to be outstanding, that's why we're all here in this room. In fact, I have been in your position before and it wasn't until my mentor helped me see a bigger reason for growing that I decided to take him up on that. I can see that your kids and your wife are a big enough reason for growing. I can see that investing in your future and their future will make you happy. It's obvious how much you love them. You can see how investing in a course that will show you how to make $100,000 in a month will help pay for the college education, can't you? In fact, with a month like that, your wife wouldn't have to work anymore, would she? At the end of the day, you don't have to buy because no one is selling you. It's your choice. If you don't want to do it, don't do it."

Notice how I tell him, "Don't do it." This will make him want to do it even more. When I tell him to buy, he resists and does the opposite. What do you think will happen when I tell him not to buy? He will do the opposite and buy. This is a very powerful strategy.

At this point, he can't say no. He told me about his life situation. I'm not here to change his life situation; I'm here to help him change his life. That's what a salespreneur does!!!!

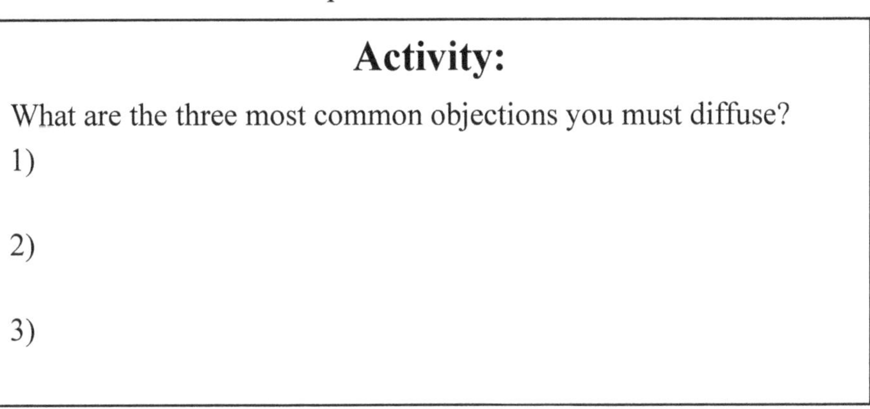

Activity:

What are the three most common objections you must diffuse?

1)

2)

3)

Preparation Habit #8: What do you want them to do?

"Wisdom is knowing what to do next, skill is knowing how to do it and virtue is doing it." - David Starr Jordan

At the end of your client meeting, what are the three things you want them to do? As we spoke earlier, this is your product and you know the action steps that clients must take to enroll or buy. Make sure that you know exactly what you want them to do when you show up to the meeting. Of course it will vary from client to client *and* you should know in advance the steps they need to take *and* make sure that you are crystal clear about it in your meeting. Always have a strong bias for action. All salespreneurs do!

What do you want them to do?

a) <u>Take action today and start implementing the tools.</u>

For you to get the results you want from this course, I want you to take the tools and implement them as fast as possible. In fact, right now, as we go through these exercises, you are preparing for your next meeting, so I already have you taking action.

b) Practice on your relationships.

In your next client meeting it will be impossible for you not to use these tools. By doing the exercise now, you are embedding in your subconscious mind what you want your clients to do. The tools are working already. Continue to practice these tools with your relationships. When I was still with New York Life, every Monday morning for four hours we would have our organization come in and role play our client process. Practice is critical to your success. I started doing seminars when I was 21. I was very nervous before my seminars *and* I would practice the day of my seminar for seven or eight hours straight. That doesn't include the time I spent weeks before the seminar, that's just the day of.

This doesn't mean that I never screwed up in my life. When I was 23, I had to give a demo workshop in front of a CPA firm for ten CPA's. We were selling them on working with our organization and having us do workshops for their clients. After a long weekend of partying and a triple espresso *and* all the workout supplements I had in my body at the time, I got up there and drew a blank. When I lost my train of thought, I began to break out in a terrible sweat. It was quite embarrassing. Two weeks later that CPA firm was coming to a presentation I was doing for 80 people. I practiced for countless hours and made sure I was well rested. I nailed it *and* delivered a mind blowing presentation! It's okay to screw up. But, Practice, Practice, Practice.

"I play to win, practice or a real game. I will not let anything get in the way of me and my competitive enthusiasm to win." - Michael Jordan

c) Tell everyone how great this product is.

To me, you are this product. You are this book. Once you start using these processes with your clients and get results, you will be a walking billboard for my book. When you are successful with these tools, you will want to tell everyone how great they are. Strategically, I have thought out what I want you to do so it has the biggest impact for you. When it impacts you, it impacts my success. That makes for a powerful relationship.

Remember what influence is: putting other peoples desires before your own and in the end both of your desires are met.

Activity:

What do you want your next client to do?

1)

2)

3)

Preparation Habit #9: What makes your product the BEST?

"Doing the best at this moment puts you in the best place for the next moment." - Oprah Winfrey

It's critical to know and believe this going into a client meeting. Once you have taken the time to reflect on what makes you unique, you will naturally share it with people. It's fun to be unique and different.

a) *Never Be Closing* is a revolution in thought.

I believe that before you decide to create anything, you must decide what the mission and purpose behind creating is. I asked myself three questions in creating this book:

1) What's missing?
2) What do people want?
3) What's the problem?

What's missing is simple. What's missing is an approach to sales and clients that is real. People all over are waking up to the fact that somewhere along the line business became about business rather than people. What's missing is a new way of thinking about business and clients. When we begin to think differently about our careers and the meaning we truly want to have, we will begin to change the way we go about our lives.

That's what people want. They want a relationship that inspires them to think bigger and grow bigger *and* someone who will hold them to their own higher standard. That higher standard is about living a fulfilling career and getting the results we deserve.

The problem is most people don't know what that standard is for their lives. As a salespreneur when you help people see the best for their lives, they won't accept anything less *and* that includes the best products. The problem is most sales processes don't do what we are doing here. People are closing their clients and clients don't want to be closed. Hence, *Never Be Closing.* This book is about holding you to your own higher standard and about helping clients develop a new standard for their lives.

Activity:

Answer these questions for yourself:

1) What's missing in your industry?

2) What do people want?

3) What's the problem?

b) Ted McGrath's experience, passion and love for helping people.

I realize that I am my product. One of the things you are buying is my experience and knowledge in sales and influence. You are also buying a process that has a 25-year track record of success behind it. For 25 years, my partner and mentor has been in the insurance business; his mentor has been in the business for 40 years. I have been in sales for the last 11 years. We have been coached by the biggest and best coaching programs in the world. We have trained thousands of sales people on mastering sales and influence. We ran an organization with 120 sales professionals in Orlando, Florida and turned down the promotion opportunity to run an organization with 300 sales professionals in Cleveland, Ohio. We understand sales and influence at a core level; it is our nature. We are always inspiring and influencing others to take action. It's not what we do, it's who we are.

I am a person who inspires others to make lasting changes in any area of their personal or professional life. It's who I am! The processes I teach have been time tested and innovated over the last several decades. We have all made millions of dollars with these processes. Use them, they work!!

c) *Never Be Closing* is transformational.

As I shared earlier, a salespreneur doesn't just change a life situation by selling a product. *A salesprenuer changes a life by selling desires and vision.* These processes will literally change how you view your own life, how you view your clients and how you view the entire world. This is a strong claim and I'm standing by it. *Never Be Closing* isn't another sales book, it is transformational - not only for your clients, but for *your* life. As you go through this book you will be performing exercises that can truly help you change your life.

In the next chapter "The Mystery Behind Why Some Clients Buy and Others Walk," you will learn how to make a deep and lasting change in anyone's life. Not only will you get people to BUY, you will gain a deep understanding of why people do the things they do. Since the chapter is coming up, I won't spoil it. You will see why my sales process is more unique then anything you have ever seen.

Activity:

What makes your product the BEST?

1)

2)

3)

Anything you do in life, you must know you're MAP.

MAP stands for:

- **Master**: You commit to mastering knowledge in this area
- **Ability**: Your have the ability to make the biggest impact
- **Passion**: You have a complete love and passion for it

If one of these is off, you are lost. That's why it's your MAP. It keeps you focused in the right direction and you always know your way. Do you commit to Mastery? Do you have the Ability? Do you have Passion for it? If either of these are a "no," then don't do it.

Preparation Habit #10: What three stories can every customer relate to?

"Stories are the creative conversion of life itself into a more powerful, clearer, more meaningful experience. They are the currency of human contact." - Robert McKee

Sharing a powerful story is a great way to diffuse an objection and inspire people to take action. It doesn't always have to be a story that brings people to tears. Make it a story that people can relate to and once they hear the story, they will easily be able to empathize and identify with the person you are talking about. Notice the stories I shared earlier about my co-worker Scott and William Wallace of "Braveheart." I shared my story and my experience at New York Life. You become the character you are hearing about.

Stories can also be a powerful way to gain credibility. Stories are also a great way to end a meeting because people remember stories. I will share many more stories with you and I have shared some already.

Just take a moment and complete the exercise below with the stories that you would like to share in your next client meeting.

- Is it a story to diffuse objections?
- Is it a story to build your credibility?
- Is it a story that evokes emotion in your client?

All the above stories are good categories to focus on because they all will inspire your clients to trust you and want to buy from you. Know your outcome and share a story based on what you want your outcome to be.

Activity:

What three stories do you know that your customers relate to?

1)

2)

3)

These are like your bag of toys. You pull them out whenever you need them. Always be prepared to share one when a client brings up an objection. A money related story is always a good one.

Preparation Habit #11: Who can they introduce you to?

"The way to gain a good reputation is to endeavor to be what you desire to appear." - Socrates

Your business cannot thrive unless you are being introduced to new relationships. This is very easy to do. Let me teach you a simple technique.

Take some time before you show up to the next meeting and jot down people that you know your clients are connected with. Once you do a great job for them and they buy, don't just ask them who they know. Tell them that you wanted to meet with Joe for a while and you know that they have a relationship with him. Would they be comfortable introducing the two of you? It's that simple. Always ask to meet new people, even if your client doesn't have a close relationship with the people you want to meet with. A new connection is better than no connection.

The next thing to do is have a generic introduction letter which you will email to them and ask them to send it for you to their relationships on your behalf. This should be a simple letter (a paragraph will suffice) talking about who you are and what you can do for others. It's simply something so when you call to make the client appointment they may have some recollection of hearing your name. However, don't wait till Christmas for your client to get around to sending the email. Speed is KING! Use your intuition and judgment on whether or not you need to wait for the letter to be sent.

Activity:

Who can your next client introduce you to?

1)

2)

3)

During the client meeting, this is how you ask to be introduced to their relationships.

Part 1: "Joe, I have a few people that you need to meet. They are incredible people and here is what you have in common with them. (Provide some information.) Would you like me to make an introduction?"

Part 2: "Joe, if you remember how I approached you, I simply asked to get together to see if there was some synergy between us and to see if we could help one another. I really value meeting with people like you. I know of your friend Sam, but I have never met him. I've heard great things and I would like to meet with him sometime. I know that only good things can come from meeting great people. Would you be open to introducing the two of us?"

Part 3: "I have a couple more people that you know who I would like to meet. Would you be open to sharing their email address and contact info with me. I'm going to send a simple email introducing myself. Is it okay if I do that and mention your name? You don't need to call them. A simple email from you or even just an email from me will probably suffice. If I don't hear from them I will let you know."

Notice my strategy of adding value to them first and then asking them to add value back. This can be done in a first meeting with anyone or in a meeting where they have already purchased something from you. Either way works because your approach to their friends is very non-threatening. Why wait until they are a client? The world's moving even if you aren't and you are going to miss out if you move slowly.

The Power of Preparation Template Assignment:

Here is a "Power of Preparation Template" for your next client meeting. Use it for all your client meetings. This should be your Sales Bible. Never go to a client meeting without doing this. This is how you will get 90% of your results in advance.

What do you already know about them?

a.
b.
c.

How do You want them to feel?

a.
b.
c.

What must they know?

a.
b.
c.

What do you want them to imagine (benefits of product)?

a.
b.
c.

What will it cost them if they don't act now?

a.
b.
c.

What will they gain if they do act now?

a.
b.
c.

What objections must you diffuse?

a
b
c

What do you want them to do?

a.

b.

c.

What makes your product the BEST?

a.

b.

c.

What three stories can every customer relate to?

a.

b.

c.

Who can they introduce you to?

a.

b.

c.

Chapter 3

The Mystery Behind Why Some Clients Buy and Others Walk

"He who has a 'why' to live can bear almost any 'how'." - Friedrich Nietzsche

Objectives:

- Understanding your Five Fundamental needs.
- Understanding your Client's Five Fundamental needs.
- A new skill set for asking simple, yet powerful questions.

In Chapter 2 we talked about the power of preparation and why it's important to anticipate how your customers are going to respond and what they are thinking in advance. Now, let's go even deeper to understand why some clients BUY and others WALK. What inspires your clients to take action, and how can you contribute to helping them get exactly what they want?

For my entire life I have been intrigued with what inspires people to do and behave in the manner they do. For years I was curious about my own behavior. Why did I practice relentlessly as a child to master a certain task; something as simple as learning how to whistle or learning how to hit a baseball? Today I wonder what causes us to do the things we do and make the decisions we make. What causes a client to take action and buy now, rather than walk out that door? Could it be that understanding what inspires clients to buy is much easier than you might have thought? Let's explore this further in this chapter.

Part I - What and Why? Desires and Needs

If you want to master the secret to sales and influencing others you must understand this:

1) *What* someone wants from his life is based on his desires.
2) *Why* someone wants it is based on fulfilling his needs.

You could also say that:

"The What" is the Vision for someone's life.
and
"The WHY" is the Purpose behind someone's life.

Wow! That's simple, yet profound.

Let's use something very common. There are a lot of people out there who desire to have $1,000,000. This is a desire they have and perhaps you have it too. It is a vision for their life. We get inspired by our desires and we get excited about them. But what is it that really drives someone or causes them to TAKE ACTION on that desire? Let's walk through this together.

Let's assume you want a million dollars. (If you don't, then insert something else.) Why do you want a million dollars? What's the purpose behind it?

Some people will tell you:

- "To be happy."
- "To feel accomplished."
- "To take care of my family."
- "To give my wife everything she deserves."
- "To travel the world and live first class."

Those are all reasons people give you, but there is an underlying force behind the reasons that drives the human spirit. It is something as basic as our NEEDS.

Strap yourselves in for this journey, my friends; this is one heck of a realization when you understand these fundamental truths.

Before you understand what drives and inspires others, you must first understand what drives you. When you understand your Model of the World and WHY you make the decisions you do, you will realize the incredible power behind the process shared in this chapter. This will open you up to a world that gives you a completely new perspective on your life. It's as if you had blurry vision one moment and all of a sudden you now have perfect 20/20 vision. Having this clarity in your life will bring tremendous clarity to your understanding of human beings and why we do the things we do. And wouldn't you like to have this type of understanding in a client meeting? Understanding the client's model of the world will allow you to tap into the driving forces behind all his decisions. I call this the "Five Fundamental and Fulfillment Needs".

This stems from Maslow's "Hierarchy of Human Needs," which is a theory of psychology he submitted in 1943. Many of you have heard of Maslow's theory. Perhaps it is just something you remember from grade school, or a psych course and you never knew its real application in today's world.

Are you ready for this breakthrough? Let's discover the driving forces behind all of your decisions and all of your relationships', right now. Let's answer the lifelong question: Why do I do what I do? Why do you do what you do? Why do people do the things they do?

Part II - The Five Fundamental and Fulfillment Needs, aka the Triple F Needs

The first four needs are called *fundamental needs*. No matter what, all of us find a way to meet these needs. Good or bad, we find a way and we must meet these needs. They are fundamental to everything we do.

The fifth and final need is the *fulfillment need*. If we don't find a way to meet this need, we will never be fulfilled in our lives.

IMPORTANT: THE WAY YOU GO ABOUT MEETING THE FIRST FOUR NEEDS WILL ULTIMATELY DETERMINE WHETHER YOU MEET THE FIFTH NEED AND LIVE A FULFILLED LIFE. (I will explain more about this later in the chapter.)

Let me pre-frame this for you. As you read about the Triple F Needs, pay attention for the two needs YOU value the most. This is important. Everyone has two needs they value the most. As you work with your clients, you want to focus in on what two needs are driving them because those two needs are the WHY behind their decision making process. Those two needs will get them to buy. After we go through the five needs, I will share with you the questions to determine anyone's needs in less than 3-5 minutes.

One more thing: Before we jump into The Triple F Needs, I want to remind you of the definition of influence. Here is the Golden Nugget:

What is Influence?

1) "If you want to inspire someone to take action, you must know what already inspires them." Think about how profound that is. If you already know what inspires someone, they are more likely to take action on the very product or service that you are offering.
2) Influence is putting other people's desires before your own and in the end both your desires are met. When you are focused on the desires of your relationship or your customers, rather than your desires, they are more likely to take action.

Now let's jump into The Triple F Needs, which will take your skill set to a completely new level in sales and influence. This model will completely change the way you view the world and it will give you a new found confidence to be successful in any relationship or any client situation. In just a short amount of time, you will know something that very few people in the world know_and you will be empowered for huge success. This is just the beginning. You can change your whole world and the world of others. You are about to experience massive results in your business.

Let's go back to our earlier example of why someone wants a $1,000,000? What's the driving force behind someone wanting $1,000,000? Or, maybe we should ask: Why would someone want/do anything in his life? What is his driving force behind wanting/doing anything?

The answer is that everyone's reason WHY could be different; but every person does what he does to meet at least one of these five needs, if not all five needs.

The Five Fundamental and Fulfillment Needs

1) **Safety**: Meeting your basic food, shelter, and survival needs
2) **Variety**: Keeping Life Fresh and Exciting
3) **Relationship**: Love, Belonging
4) **Respect**: Self-esteem and Feeling Important
5) **Life Purpose**: Fulfilling One's Potential, Contribution to Others

The First Fundamental Need: Safety

"Those who would give up essential Liberty, to purchase a little temporary Safety, deserve neither Liberty nor Safety." - Benjamin Franklin

I agree with Ben here, that we should never give up our liberty for safety. Although safety is still a fundamental need all humans have. Some value safety too much and they give up the liberty that every person deserves. I value freedom WAY more than safety. But some people, perhaps even your clients, have learned to value safety above all things. Let's explore this.

WHY is safety a driving need? Let's start by sharing the basics here. Every single person on the planet must have his basic food, shelter and survival needs met. This is obvious. Even a homeless person finds a way to live, and under those conditions his focus is on finding food and shelter for the day. If someone can't meet his basic safety needs he isn't going to be focused on the other four needs. Let's get beyond basic food and shelter and talk about examples of how people go about meeting their safety needs as it relates more to your clients and your relationships. If your clients don't feel safe about your product, none of the other features of the product matter.

Here is the secret: we all find a way to meet our safety needs, but we all value safety in a very different way. SAFETY IS A NEED and if you don't have it you will find a way to meet that need. What keeps life interesting is that we all have different ways of meeting this need. For example:

1) Do you know the kind of person who, before he goes on vacation, checks the door locks 15 times, makes sure he packed 15 suit cases and checks his flight status ten times before he leaves the house? Okay, I'm being a little exaggerated here. But do you know the type of person I am talking about. Isn't it quite obvious that this person values safety at a high, high level? On a scale of 1-10, he values safety at an 11.

2) How about the person who picks up at a moment's notice, books a one way ticket to France, packs a tooth brush and some underwear and lets everyone know he will be back later. On a scale of 1-10, this person values safety at around a 2 or 3.

These two people have two totally different beliefs when it comes to safety and this is the key distinction here. The way they value safety and make their decisions on travel stems from what they BELIEVE about the world. (We will talk about beliefs in a bit.)

How important is it in a sales situation to understand if your client values safety or not? I can tell you: on a scale of 1-10, it's an 11. This will make you aware of how often you talk about the guarantees of your product in your client meeting. If your client is the person who packs 15 suit cases, then you better make sure you discuss the guarantees and that you bring it up several times.

At the end of my meeting with a client, before I get into the solution, I address his safety need. "By the way Sally, before I share some incredible ideas with you, I want you to know that I guarantee my work" and then I share the guarantees with her. I have different guarantees for different products. For my last sales course, I guaranteed a refund if they weren't happy with the course. What guarantees or safety features can you add to your product?

Question: How do you discover if they are a "15 suit case packer?" In other words, how do you discover if your client's driving need is safety?

Answer: Through simple conversations and strategic questions that I will share with you soon. I call it "The Needs Conversation or Needs Questions." These Questions will help you determine someone's driving needs in 3-5 minutes.

I was recently dealing with a client who balances his checkbook and follows every single penny. It made sense for me to offer the payment plan option right off the bat because this would make my client feel SAFE that everything is on schedule and he was not biting off more than he could chew. Of course with him, I stressed the guarantees of the product. These are also the same kind of people who are going to stress out if something goes wrong with your product, so be prepared.

Every client wants safety or guarantees to some degree. The key is to know whether safety is the primary factor that will get your client to buy. For me personally, safety or guarantees aren't the primary factor. How about you?

The Second Fundamental Need: Variety

"Sameness is the mother of disgust, variety the cure." - Petrarca Petrarch (1304 - 1374)

How important do you think it is to know if your client values variety? If you could determine in a few minutes whether or not your client values variety, do you think your sales would go up?

We all want life to be fresh and exciting don't we? That's the spice and variety of life. Do you have anybody in your life who was born in New Jersey, grew up in one house, never moved out of that house, might even still live with their parents, has had the same job for their entire life_and has never left their hometown except to go to the Jersey Shore on a holiday? Okay, I'm using the Jersey example because I was born there, but you know what I mean. On a scale of 1-10, these folks value variety at a 1. This doesn't mean they don't find other ways to meet their variety needs. Perhaps they watch lots of movies in the same house where they grew up in and that's enough variety for them.

In my hometown, most of the kids from my high school graduated high school, looked at colleges on the east coast, graduated college, went to New York City to find a career and eventually settled back down in the suburbs to raise a family, right next to their parents, in the same town they grew up. Do you think there is a little bit of a SAFETY habit that's recurring here which helps all of these people and families to meet their safety needs? I'm willing to bet that some of these people would be overwhelmed if you gave them a lot of different choices in a client meeting. They just aren't used to variety.

I, on the other hand, went to college where no one else from my high school was going and I now live on the West Coast. I value variety a bit more then my childhood friends. How about you?

However, we all need some variety. In fact, I'm willing to bet that my childhood friends probably wouldn't like to eat Ritz crackers and caviar every day for a month because they would get sick of it. Actually let's take away the caviar because that would be too big of a leap for some of them. But even for them, the Ritz crackers would get old after 30 days. The point is we all need some variety in our lives, otherwise we would feel like we are the walking dead. Without some variety we would be bored and totally unfulfilled!

Tonight I had dinner with my friend Jeff and he told me that he gets offended when someone is boring and isn't open to new things. He literally gets offended. Here's a guy who was born in Arkansas, lived in Ohio for several years, went to college in Boulder, Colorado, joined the Peace Corp, moved to California, became a stock broker, bought a million dollar condo that he couldn't afford, quit his job, moved to L.A. to become an actor, slept on his friends couches, declared bankruptcy, got selected for a reality TV show in Dubai, lived there for nine months, became an accountant afterwards and now lives in Cincinnati with his mom, taking college courses for his second degree, in journalism. Is this a guy who has a driving need for variety or what! Some of us go to the beach on weekends for variety and he travels the world and changes jobs like its underwear.

This one takes the cake! Jeff just sent me an email the other day. He thought it would be fascinating to write his obituary. Now, I know for certain that Jeff loves variety. He is a dear friend of mine and he literally is the spice of life. You always have a good time with my dear friend Jeff Hoskins. Love you Jeff!

Question: How would you work with Jeff in a sales situation?

Answer: In a sales situation, it would be important to offer Jeff the FARM. If you are selling cars, you better show the JEFFS all the models on the lot, all the different colors and every possibility, otherwise they are likely to go exploring on your competitor's car lot. In fact, you better show Jeff the cars that haven't even come out yet.

If you knew that your client valued variety and you could figure this out in a few minutes, do you think you would improve the odds of getting him as a client?

Start thinking about all your client presentations. Wouldn't it make sense to highlight the variety of your products in your presentation? If you have no idea who your audience is, it makes sense to touch on variety because it is a need that every person has; some more than others, but everyone still needs variety.

Activity:

Think of your last client.

1) If you had to guess, on a scale of 1-10, how much did they value variety?
2) If it was a 10, did you tailor your presentation towards that driving need?
3) What could you have improved, knowing what you know now?

What variety does your product/service provide for someone? Write it down now.

The Third Fundamental Need: Relationship: Is about Love, Belonging

"Poets and mystics have been telling us for centuries: Wake up. Wake to your true self. Wake to your own connections to what is around you right now. Gaze into someone's eyes and discover who looks back. Penetrate the mysteries where the worlds touch. Don't go back to sleep." - Paul H. Ray, Sherry Ruth Anderson

Why is Relationship a Fundamental Need? We all need love, a feeling of belonging and connection to others. We are human beings who NEED relationships. If we are left alone when we are born without any physical contact, we will die. Relationship is critically important in our lives. The quality of our conversations determines the quality of our relationships *and* the quality of our relationships determines the quality of our lives.

How do you go about meeting your relationship needs? Do you like having thousands of friends across the world that you can connect with anytime you please? Is that how you fulfill your needs for relationship, by belonging to a group of friends who make you feel connected? Or, do you go about meeting your relationship needs by having two very close friends and these two friends make you feel loved and connected in ways you could never imagine? Do you have lots of pets and they meet your relationship needs? Do you have lots of kids and they meet your relationship needs?

Different strokes for different folks! All of this is based on our views and beliefs about life and relationships. Don't you think it would be good to understand your clients' viewpoints on life and relationships, because this will ultimately determine what needs they value most, which will ultimately determine whether or not they buy from you?

At this point you may want to ask yourself: What do I believe about relationships?

Is one of the prior examples better than the other? Absolutely not.

Question: What's the reason that we all meet our needs in a different way?

Answer: Our beliefs - the way we see the world.

We were born in different places, raised by different parents, inherited different genes, lived in different cultures *and* spent time with different people. We have knelt at different graves, been held in different arms and loved different people. Therefore, each one of us has a model of the world that is unique. How we see the world determines how we will go about fulfilling all our needs, which includes our relationship needs.

Let me share another example:

1) Do you know anyone in your life who is a total drama queen/king in his/her relationships? She jumps up and down and makes such a big deal out of everything because this is how she gets the attention she needs from her relationships?
2) On the flip side, do you know someone who is completely loving and giving and is constantly focused on making the other person happy? This is how she meets her relationship needs.

In a client meeting, how do you think you focus the meeting with the drama king? You focus on him. In a relationship with you as a sales entrepreneur, he wants your attention. You give him all the attention and you let him know how this product or service is going to impact him and make his entire life better. (Side note: Most of these people will be high maintenance.)

As you think about your ideal clients, pick them well, because this is your life and you get to decide whom you want to have a lasting relationship with. The money is never worth the headache. Do you remember the two friends who gave me 20 million dollars to manage for them? It wasn't a great decision on my part. They were very high maintenance and it was a constant headache.

Question: In a client meeting, how do you think you focus the meeting with the loving, caring client?

Answer: You focus on the people he loves and cares about. Why? Because if the people he loves and cares about are happy because of the product your client purchased, then your client feels fulfilled. Why would this fulfill him? Simple, he was responsible for making his family/friends happy and that fulfills his relationship need.

Are you starting to understand how important it is to understand your client's needs?

Activity:

How do you go about fulfilling your relationship needs? Take a moment and write it down.

When you buy things, are you thinking of others more or are you thinking of yourself?
(It's okay, be honest!)

In your next client meeting, notice how your clients talk about their relationships. If they are talking about their family, then you know what direction to go. If they are talking about themselves then you know what direction to go.

Here is a simple, yet powerful question to help you determine your clients driving needs: What is important about relationships to you?

This question may seem like it's for an in-depth client conversation. You might be thinking, you don't just walk up and ask someone this in a casual conversation. I will show you how to ask this question when we get to the "Needs Questions." More importantly, I will show you how to weave it into any conversation. There are many ways to ask the same question, depending on the situation.

Or, another approach would be: Tell me about your family. Would this (product) mean a lot to your family?

If your client focuses the direction on his family, then you know RELATIONSHIP is a driving need for him. If he focuses the attention back on himself, then most likely that leads us to:

The Fourth Fundamental Need: Respect

"I'm not the greatest; I'm the double greatest. Not only do I knock 'em out; I pick the round." -Muhammad Ali

Can you take a wild guess which one of Muhammad Ali's driving needs was? I'm willing to bet it was respect and feeling important. I'm sure there are other needs he values but just the way he communicates and his mannerisms lead me to believe that he likes feeling important and recognized.

Everyone in the world has a need to feel significant and important. Some people want to be admired and respected by the entire world, while others just want to feel respected and important in the eyes of their family. We all need respect on some level and we all find a way to meet it. In Dale Carnegie's bestselling book, "How to Win Friends and Influence People," he highlights the fact that everyone wants to feel appreciated and important.

Example:

1) Some people build their entire lives around achieving, winning awards, advancing professionally, or being the CEO of a major company. These types of people value respect in a BIG way. You could say that it is their # 1 driving need. And doing all this is how they go about fulfilling their need for respect.

   Now remember, we all have a need for respect *and* we all have different ways of meeting our respect needs.

2) Another person could get his respect by joining a gang and holding people up at gun point to feel he is respected in the world. This may not be the way you meet your needs, but GOOD or BAD, people will find a way to feel respected in this world.

Are both people meeting their respect need at a high level? Yes.

Now, if you have a client in your office and he has respect as his number one driving need, do you think it would be important to tie the benefits of your product into his respect needs?

THIS IS PRICELESS: Strap yourself in for this one, as I demonstrate HOW:

Story # 1: The 10 Million Dollar Life Insurance Man

I used to sell insurance. If I was selling someone a $10,000,000 insurance policy because I knew that he needed this amount of money to protect his family, how do you think I would go about selling this to someone who's number one driving need is RESPECT? People whose driving need is respect sometimes feel they are larger than life and they will never die or they don't want to think about death. So why on earth would I talk to this person about dying, when that isn't his concern? Pay attention! He is here in the office because any person of respect is not going to leave his family without life insurance, but to get him to buy what he SHOULD; I have to tap into his driving need, respect. If I tap into the part of him that wants to leave money for his family, he may only walk out of there with $5,000,000 of life insurance. If I tap into his respect need as it pertains to him, GUARANTEED he walks out with $10,000,000 of life insurance. Here is how it's done.

(Side Note: I am not tricking this guy to buy more. As a professional, I know what kind of insurance someone in his situation SHOULD have.)

Me: "Joe, I know you're here because you love your family, that's a given. Before I give you what you want, I just wanted to share with you the guidelines behind purchasing this life insurance. In fact, there is actually a limit to the amount of insurance someone can buy. EVEN for a guy who is as successful as you. (His ears just perked up.)

"Did you know there was a limit?" (First off, a guy who is RESPECTED and SUCCESSFUL doesn't like anyone telling him there's a limit. He got to where he's at by dismissing all limits.)

Joe: "No, I didn't know that."

Me: "Yeah, you actually have to qualify for something called your 'Human Life Value.' Your 'human life value' is determined by your age, assets and income *and* then the insurance company puts a value on your life. For example, did you know that only wealthy people can qualify for a $10,000,000 life insurance policy?"

Joe's response: "No." (95% of the time.)

Me: "Yeah, they're not going to sell it to your average guy coming off the street. You really have to be a successful person to even be considered for this. I'm not saying you are going to buy $10,000,000, Joe. All I'm saying is we should find out what your 'human life value' is and then make a decision from there. Based on what you shared with me, I'm sure your "human life value" is easily at $10,000,000. Would you like to find out?"

In that meeting, or if necessary, by the next meeting, I calculate it for him *and* I tell him, "I know that you are going to be worth a hundred million someday, your 'human life value' just came back at $10,000,000. A guy at your level of success should definitely have $10,000,000 of coverage. All my wealthy clients take this first initial step. In fact Joe, I'm going to creatively show you how to pay for it with no money out of your pocket, even though it's a very small premium of about $400-500 per month, for a $10,000,000 policy on your life. You can see how this could benefit you, can't you? Does this make sense?"

Right now I am making Joe feel important so he can feel respected and special. In fact, to get Joe to spend money on a $10,000,000 of insurance, you just need to get him to feel like he is worth 100 million dollars and he won't flinch at writing the check for a $10,000 premium. The feeling of importance he gains is outweighing the cost of the insurance. Very interesting, huh? In fact, it's totally kick ass, isn't it?

You can see that I am not closing Joe here. I'm not scaring him with tactics that he is going to die. I'm not telling him that he has to do this because when he passes away he has an obligation to his family. He knows he is going to die one day; he knows he has a family. He is an intelligent guy. I want to appeal to what makes him feel great and what is most important to him. If walking around and feeling like he is worth $10,000,000 is what makes him feel important. Then, I know that's what I need to focus on.

The entire life insurance industry used to always focus on making wealthy people buy large life insurance policies to pay their estate taxes at death. They were closing people and forcing them to buy into a general product they assumed the client needed and wanted. My point to you is not to ever assume anything. When you assume that someone should buy something for general reasons, he will feel like you are trying to close him. Even if I know someone should have a large life insurance policy because he is wealthy, I want to look for the reason of why he would want to have that policy, not my reason or the industry's reason.

In what ways does your industry try to generalize why someone needs to buy something? Be aware of these generalizations and use the needs conversation to get specific with your clients.

How do you determine if someone's driving need is respect? I will share the Needs Conversation/Questions to ask later in this chapter.

<u>Story # 2: The Story of Scott's Parents</u>

I told you earlier part of the story about my friend Scott. Although this story isn't about selling per se, these tools we learn about help change people's lives as well. Remember what I said in the beginning of the book. Sales people change people's life situations and salespreneurs change people lives. BIG DIFFERENCE! This is truly my passion. Imagine the impact you will have changing peoples' lives, one person at a time. As Margaret Meade once said, "Never doubt that a small group of committed citizens can change the world, indeed it is the only thing that ever has." Amen, Margaret!!!!!!

Let me share with you a simple conversation that changed Scott's life.

Earlier I shared that Scott's parents both died within months of each other in their 60's. Scott is the type of person and son that values relationship *and* is so incredibly genuine and loyal to the people he cares about. Scott also has a brother and three sisters. Scott and his other siblings were self-sufficient, successful *and* managed their money well - except for the brother. To condense this story, let's just say that Scott's brother was always finding a way to get money from the parents. His whole life was lived relying on his parents for money. In fact, he would do wild things that you wouldn't even believe to get money from his father.

It got to the point where his father was fed up with this son, but he couldn't say no. Now, when Scott's mother passed, his father changed the reading of the will. All the money was supposed to be divided among the kids equally. When it came time for reading of the will, can you believe that the wild brother received five times more money than Scott and his sisters? Imagine this knowing that Scott came over every day to take care of his parents and this brother hardly ever showed up. And, here Scott and his sisters are at the will reading feeling like they were totally shafted.

This weighed on Scott's and his sisters' minds for over a year. It wasn't the money that they received that hurt them, it was the feeling that they were the good children and they couldn't understand why their parents would treat them differently.

I asked Scott one question, after I explained the Five Human Needs to him:

Me: "Was one of your dad's top two needs respect?" (I already knew the answer.)

Scott: "Yes, it was."

Me: "Of course every father wants the respect of his son. In fact, it sounds like your one brother felt like he was entitled to the money that your Dad kept giving him."

Scott: "Yes, yes. (Anxious.) He showed up while they were on their death bed and said it was his birth right to have the family inheritance."

Me: "How do you think that made your father feel? He's about to leave this earth and after all he's done for his son, it's still not enough. He's about to leave this earth knowing that his son won't love him or respect him if he doesn't take care of him with the inheritance.

"The other side of this Scott is that your father always had your love and respect up until the end, didn't he? It was unconditional. Your father knew your love for him and respect would never change."

Scott: "Holy shit! I can't believe what you just made me realize. I have to share this with my sisters. He gave the money to my brother because he needed to know that he respected him and still loved him with his last breath on this earth. That was the only way my brother would respect him. I GET IT!"

You see, these NEEDS are so powerful that we will do anything to fulfill them even if they don't make logical sense. The model I am sharing with you helps you take something irrational and make it rational. Now you are able to make sense out of all situations in your life, especially your clients, but more importantly, the people you love.

At this point, I know you can't wait to get the few simple questions that help you determine what someone's top two needs are. I am going to give them to you right after we go through the fifth and final need, "Life's Purpose."

By now you realize that making your client feel important and appreciated throughout your entire presentation and meeting is fundamental to your success. Everyone wants to feel important, everyone! It's your role to figure out which client's value it the most and then to focus your energy on their respect need.

Review: Up until this point, we have discussed four fundamental needs. These needs are fundamental because we all find a way to meet the first four. The ways we go about fulfilling these needs aren't always positive driving forces in our lives; however we will do whatever it takes to meet these needs. As human beings they are fundamental and essential to our lives. Now you know how your clients make decisions in their lives.

Now, let me explain the NEED that everyone searches for and only the purposeful ones really ever fulfill. This is why I call this the "fulfillment need." We can all figure out a way to be happy. Happiness is a state. A new car, you're happy. A promotion, you're happy. A fun birthday party, you're happy. If you're in a bad mood right now, think about a time when you were happy. Does your mood change? Yes, it does. You can be happy any time you want. Fulfillment, on the other hand, is something that endures and emerges out of our driving need to have a Grand Purpose to our lives.

I call this the **Fifth and Final Fulfillment Need: Life's Purpose**:

"The Greatest Tragedy in Life isn't death; it's what we allow to die inside ourselves while we are still living." - Norman Cousins

"Life is a promise; fulfill it." - Mother Theresa

I want to go back to a point that I made in the beginning of the chapter that is very important. The way you go about meeting your first four needs will ultimately determine whether or not you meet the Fifth and Final Fulfillment Need. The Fulfillment Need, aka Life's Purpose, is 100% about living to your full potential, growing and contributing to others. Every person on the planet has a desire to grow and contribute to others, but how does someone actually do this if he is coming from a difficult place in his life?

1) For example, if you are barely paying your bills or eating, how much can you really be focused on contributing to the lives of others? You can't because you aren't meeting your safety needs.
2) If you are on drugs and high all the time, are you growing as a person? No, you are shrinking as a human being. The drugs are meeting your variety needs, but you aren't moving forward in life.
3) If you are consistently having relationship problems and the drama never stops in your life because you don't feel loved, how much can you really love and contribute to others. Are you really growing by creating drama in this relationship or are you just playing games? The truth is you're playing games. Even though you are meeting your relationship needs because you are getting the attention you need, you still aren't making progress in your life. You can only love and contribute to others as much as you love and contribute to yourself.
4) If you are monetarily successful in business and you feel important and respected, but you lied and cheated to achieve that success, eventually you will get caught. It's pretty hard to contribute to others when you are cheating them. It's pretty hard to grow in life when you will eventually lose everything as a result of unethical behavior. Yes, this person is meeting his respect need *and* it comes at a cost to his life's progress.

The point I am making here is that some people meet their needs at a high level but in a way that is damaging to their progress in life and in a way that comes at a tremendous cost.

Question: How likely is it for someone in the above scenarios to meet the fifth and final fulfillment need?

Answer: Not likely at all. Unless this person changes his view of the world, changes his behaviors and changes his beliefs, he will never be fulfilled in his life. WHY? In all the scenarios I shared with you, those people are not growing or contributing or even close to living in their full potential, which is a prerequisite for being fulfilled.

If you are not meeting your needs in a way that is helping you make progress, then it is time to make a change. Remember, everyone finds a way to meet the first four needs; EVERYONE. The question is: will you meet these needs in a way that is beneficial to your growth and your purpose on this earth? When you are meeting your needs in a way that is beneficial and enduring, then you have an opportunity to meet the fifth and final fulfillment need.

Imagine a client walking into your office. He sits down and he is extremely well put together. Financially, you can tell this guy has made it BIG. His safety needs are taken care of. As you begin to converse with him (once you have been trained in the questions I will share with you), you discover that his relationship needs, respect needs and variety needs are all being met at a high level. He is making major progress in his life.

Pretend for a moment you are in the insurance business. As you begin to talk to this man, you realize that everything in his life is taken care of. You start to wonder, is there anything I can do for this person? You dig a bit deeper into who he really is and during your conversation you realize that he is a giver. He gives to his employees; he gives to his family; he gives to everyone. As he speaks about it, you notice that he is happy and warm when he talks about giving to others. You start to realize this guy is very much driven by his Life's Purpose. His kids are set for college; his wife has everything she could ever imagine.

Question: How do you get this person to even want to be a client and do some financial planning with you?

Answer: You talk to him about his legacy, charities he may want to give to, causes he may want to support *and* you frame your presentation and questions in a manner that touches his Fulfillment Need of Life's Purpose. Do you understand how useful the Triple F Needs are for you with clients? It's invaluable. (The questions for determining needs are coming up shortly.) It's very important for you to have a strong understanding of the Triple F Needs before you start asking questions and attempt to figure out your clients' driving needs. By now you realize these needs are what will drive your clients to BUY from you.

Activity:

Who is a person you know that is driven by The Fifth Need, Life's Purpose?

How will you talk to them now knowing that this is one of their driving needs?

Let's dive into Life's Purpose. This is a topic that truly deserves its due attention because this is WHY we are here on this earth.

<u>Story #1: The Story of One Thing</u>

I recently watched an old movie, "City Slickers" with Billy Crystal. Billy Crystal played the role of a middle aged guy with a family, stuck in an unfulfilling job. Billy's wife sent him away on a trip into the wilderness with his best friends to find his smile again. It was a ranching trip with cowboys, who were bringing in a herd of cattle. There's an awesome character in the movie named Curly. He's an old cowboy, who is confident and tough and loves being a cowboy. Here is what he says to Billy Crystal.

Curly: You know you all come up here about the same time, same age, looking for the meaning of life. What are you, about 40?

Billy: 39

Curly: Yep, you city slickers think that if you get away from it all, somehow you will take back what you had here, but it never lasts. Not until you figure out the meaning of life.

Billy: (sarcastically) And you know the meaning of life, Curly? What is it?

Curly: One thing

Billy: One thing?!

Curly: Yep, one thing.

Billy: And what is that one thing?

Curly: That's what every man has got to figure out….

I love this scene because Curly was telling Billy that when you figure out the one thing in life that fulfils you, nothing else matters. That one thing is your Life's Purpose. When you have that meaning and focus in your life, you are able to grow, contribute to others and live out your full potential. You are able to live out your destiny. That's how you live a fulfilled life.

I believe that the purpose to life is to live your purpose. When you love what you do and you can share it with others, contribute to others, belong to something bigger than yourself *and* truly make a difference in people's lives, there is no greater feeling in the world or no grander reason to live. As a salespreneur, it's not just about making sales, is it?

Some days making a sale may be all you focus on because you are worried about paying the bills or you are stressed about meeting your company goals, but the moments that truly last are the ones where you are in the moment with your customer. The moments where everything you say inspires others, everything you do is done right *and* everything you feel is that you are doing what you were born to do.

I have goose bumps just thinking about this. As my words are jumping off the page and my passion is filling your hearts, I want you to know one thing: my calling is to help you live a fulfilled and prosperous life and I will go to the grave with every last ounce of passion and inspiration to help you become a success and a master in sales and influence. You have my commitment to you. Lets Rock!

It may seem like I'm going off on a tangent here with Life's Purpose, but I'm not. This is a very important need that we all pray to fulfill. I am getting to the tools that will help you uncover your relationships needs. In fact, by now you should be able to understand the driving needs of those closest to you. Stop and reflect on your best friend's driving needs or even your spouse.

Activity:

As Curly said, "What is your one thing?"

Think about it. Everywhere in nature, things GROW or they DIE. We are no different. If we aren't growing, we merely exist. If we aren't growing, we aren't fulfilled.

Think back to a time where you were truly growing. (It could be right now!) During the time you were making progress, I'm sure you felt you were growing mentally, spiritually, physically, financially *and* you just knew there was a reason for your existence on this planet; that you were going to make a difference. What was that time for you and what were you doing?

Now, think of a time where you were serving others and contributing to the greater good. What was a moment in your life where you remember having this passion to serve, what were you doing?

Now as you think about this time where you were on top of the world *and* everything was incredible, what was the next thing you wanted to do? You wanted to share your Passions, Wisdom, Successes, Failures *and* Resources with others didn't you? This is what you do when you are fulfilled *and* this is what fulfills you as well. We all must grow and contribute to feel fulfilled in our lives. That's called Life's Purpose. It is a NEED that we all search the earth to fulfill.

Activity:

How does your product help your clients fulfill their Life's Purpose?

This would be an important benefit to figure out. When you are contributing to the Life's Purpose of another and when you provide him with meaning and direction in his life, he isn't just a client, he's a friend. And this is how you should always see clients, as your friends. In fact, let's turn a corner and start referring to your clients as friends.

By now, you understand that we all want to grow, contribute and live in our full potential, because without this we will never be fulfilled.

Story #2: The Story of Life's Higher Calling

When I was 28 years old, I remember standing on the top floor of the Suntrust building in downtown Orlando, Florida, with a life changing question echoing in my head. I was the #5 partner in New York Life out of 500 partners and I had four out of five of my needs met:

1) I had Safety - I was making plenty of money.
2) I had Variety - Every day was different; there were lots of new challenges to deal with; and the environment was interesting because we were always teaching personal development courses in the firm.
3) I had Relationship - My Business partner was my best friend *and* I worked with some great people.
4) I had Respect - I was a partner in the number one Life Insurance Company in America, leading 120 sales professionals.

I had everything but the fifth and final need, Life's Purpose. I wasn't fulfilled. What should you do when you're not fulfilled?

As I was standing there on the 29th floor, I asked myself a different question: Is this all there is?

What do I really want?

In that moment I realized there was something more. I had a higher calling. I was going to be the leader in personal/professional growth across the world. I was going to provide others with the mindset, skill set and strategies they needed to succeed in the world. I wasn't just going to do it in business; I was going to make a lasting difference in the world. I wanted a life of passion and I was willing to jump off the 29th floor of the Suntrust building and grow wings on the way down. I had a burning desire to inspire others to transform areas of their lives where they were unfulfilled. I would be the voice and the courage of others, until they found their voice. I would be the voice of change. In that moment, I left everything behind and gave up a huge promotion opportunity so I could follow my passion and live a fulfilled and meaningful life. I discovered my ONE THING. I'm sharing some of it with you in this book and I'm grateful to be here with you on your journey. I know that you are going to succeed in a BIG way.

What was the point of going on and on about Life's Purpose, The Fifth and Final Fulfillment Need?

I believe that above all things, people want to live a life of purpose. I'm not saying they are going to push their other needs to the side and go straight for life's purpose. We know that isn't the case. Here is the thing that I want you to know and really think about. A salespreneur; a person who insists on THE BEST OF TIMES; a person who "works every day to make sure that their BEST is better *and* their better is BEST," as Walter Payton once said; these types of people have a gift. You have a gift and this is why you are drawn to this. This gift comes with great responsibility and the responsibility is this:

The Salespreneur's Code:

- We MUST, we MUST take on the responsibility for helping our clients imagine a life that they never could have imagined on their own.
- We must help our clients dream their way out of their current circumstances.
- We must envision with them a new reality and a new world of possibility.

When our clients are down and out and focused on meeting their safety need of food and a roof over their heads; when they are unfocused and looking for variety in the wrong areas of their life; when they just want to be loved and connected with their relationships because all else is failing; when they only want to feel important for a moment because they want respect in their lives that they are not getting; it is our role - our privilege - to help them imagine a bigger future; one filled with promise *and* purpose *and* growth *and* potential *and* contribution. This is the life that everyone wants to live. They settle for less because they have to find a way to meet their fundamental needs.

However, all people want to be fulfilled; all people. The best salespereneur helps them imagine that bigger future, a future of possibility, where the very product/service the salespreneur is offering can help their client live a Life of Purpose. When you can help your clients imagine that, you have arrived ladies and gentlemen. There is nothing nobler on the planet. That is why I am writing this book. NO OTHER REASON! Let's do it together. In the upcoming chapter I will share the processes to help your clients imagine and achieve this type of future.

I want you to pause for a moment and write this down, post it on your wall:

"A new purpose gives a new meaning to life. A new vision can change a life." - Ted McGrath

If you can give someone a purpose to his life and a healthy reason for living, then you can truly help make a difference in his life. When you help people with a new vision in life, they can change their world and the world of everyone around them. This is the role of a salespreneur and I will be sharing an amazing process on Vision in the last chapter. Stay Tuned!

Part III: The Needs Conversation and Putting It All to Work

Now that you have taken the journey with me through the Five Fundamental and Fulfillment Needs:

1) What two needs do you value the most? As mentioned earlier, every person will have two of five needs they value the most. As a salespreneur, you will always be looking for what those two driving needs are for your clients. Their top two needs are where you will focus your attention during your presentation and conversation. This will increase your current ratio of acquiring more clients in a shorter period of time. This will reduce the sales cycle in a major way.
2) What is your biggest insight about your life now? Journal about it.

Just as I am checking in with you throughout this book, you will always be checking in with your clients throughout your conversations. It's important to know what your clients are thinking and to know where they are at in terms of their interest in your product. I will introduce you to a technique called feeling questions in the later chapters. This too will reduce your sales cycle and assist you in diffusing objections.

NOW, FINALLY, the moment you have been waiting for. It's time to introduce you to the "The Triple F Need's" questions for determining your friends' (clients') needs in a sales situation. I am about to share with you some very powerful, strategic questions, which you will use in a client situation or with any relationships. These questions are fun and you should use them all the time.

Needs Questioning: NQ

What is your NQ? You know what IQ is and now you know what NQ is. I want you to have a high skill level in your NQ or Need's Questioning.

Tips:

1) Use the NQ model in every client meeting.
2) Use this model to discover which two needs your clients/friends value the most.
3) This model will get your clients to buy and could increase your sales by a factor of ten.

Before you get into the NQ, you must have the rapport to ask the NQ in a conversational manner. I want to introduce you to a set of questions that I call Steering Questions. The purpose of a Steering Question is to build rapport and then lead the client into a more specific direction, so that you can ask them the NQ's in a conversational manner that flows.

Simple Rapport questions are:

1) What line of work are you in?
2) Where are you from?

These are the questions you ask every day to get to know people.

Once you build the rapport, transition to the Steering Questions:

1) How did you get started in your business?
2) Tell me about your family.

Where do people spend most of their time in life? Work and family, hence the previous two steering questions.

The previous two questions are very general. They are also personal enough to build more rapport with your client. The fact that the questions are general allows you to steer your client in a specific direction that is going to help them with their outcome. It is also going to help you with your outcome, which is to understand your clients' behaviors. When you understand their behaviors, you understand how to inspire them into action. Steering is a technique that you will pick up quickly. You do it in your life all the time anyway. Now is a time for you to be conscious when you are doing it.

You just asked your client about his life in an indirect way. So now when you get to the Needs Questions-NQ you ask, "What's life about these days?"

Your client isn't taken back by this question. You don't ever want your client to feel like your questions are out of line or too penetrating. You wouldn't show up to a first date and kiss your date on the mouth, would you? No, you would wait for rapport to be built. You would ask questions; you would connect on an intimate level and at the end of the night you may give her/him a kiss. At that point it would probably feel like the right thing to do and both you and your date would be comfortable because of the way the evening flowed. It's the same thing with your client meetings. You want the conversation to flow. BUT, no kiss at the end. A check is fine, but no kiss!

Here are the NQ's:

a) <u>What's life about?</u>

As I just shared above, this is a heavy question for the beginning of a conversation. This is why you use Steering Questions, which will help Steer you to the NQ's and allow the conversation to flow. If your client were to talk about his life or business for ten minutes and you said, "What's life about these days?" This question would fit in perfectly with the conversation. That's exactly how you want to ask a Needs Question. Let me show you how to weave this question in. "Joe, life has changed in the last few years for you, hasn't it? I can imagine that being a parent is very fulfilling. I'm curious, what's life about for you these days, how has your perspective on things changed?"

Notice how I make this question very conversational. I ask the question from a place of curiosity. I want to learn from Joe and about him. I'm asking for his perspective on life, which will help me uncover his belief systems. All very valuable.

b) <u>What's the meaning of relationship?</u>

For some of you, asking this question may seem too deep. So here is how you frame it so it's conversational: "What do relationships mean to you these days?" OR "What is important about relationships?"

For example, if a client starts openly telling you about his divorce, asking the previous question fits in very well. What got him talking about his divorce was probably the steering question/statement: Tell me about your family. Before you jump into some of these questions, make sure you are on the subject of relationship before you ask an NQ question about relationships.

Let me demonstrate: "Sally, I appreciate how hard you work in your business. I work the same hours as well. Tell me something, do you have a lot of good friends at the office that you spend time with? It must be tough balancing your personal and professional life."

Notice how I'm steering Sally into the relationship question. Indirectly I'm asking her about her relationships and friends. I didn't ask the exact question: What's important about relationships? But I am still learning about whether or not relationships are her driving need. That is how you weave it into a casual conversation. The truth is you have these discussions every day. They are real and authentic conversations. The problem is most sales people aren't paying attention to the underlying current of the conversation.

c) <u>What drives you?</u>

This is a great question when you are talking about the person's profession or accomplishments. "Wow, Sally. You have really been a success in a short period of time. I admire that. What drives you to work so hard and achieve like that?"

d) <u>What gets you out of bed in the morning?</u>

This question is similar to the previous question. It's just a more casual way of asking it. You will know when to use this question in a conversation.

e) <u>What are you passionate about?</u>

Let's assume you just asked a Steering Question, "How did you get started in your career?" And, now the client is telling you that he is bored with his profession and he really doesn't know what to do with his life. Asking him about his passion would be a great question. This will give you deeper insight into who he is as a person and it will be easy to pick up on the needs he values the most.

Let me demonstrate: "Jim, you have been in this career for 15 years; you must have a ton of knowledge. What do like most about your job?" (Wait for Jim's response.) "So, what are you passionate about these days?"

Needs Questions are critically important:

1) If you don't know what their needs are then you don't know your customers.
2) As you ask the NQ questions, you will be listening for what your clients believe about their life, their work and their relationships.
3) Beliefs shape a client's decision-making process. These beliefs will help you discover their driving needs.
4) Their driving needs are the force behind WHY they buy.

You can see how important the NQ's are to your success, can't you?

Think about the time you are wasting in client meetings when you could get to the core of who they are in several minutes. Once you get to that core of who they are, imagine the quality of the relationship you could truly build.

There are customers that you just sell a product to and make a few hundred dollars. There are customers that you sell a product to, make a bigger commission and you never see the person again. You now have the power to change this. You now have a tool to tap into the driving force of your client's psychology. You now know how to give your clients and get your clients exactly what they want. You know how to get your clients to BUY for their reasons. This makes for a fulfilled customer.

Now let's go deeper!

Part IV: How Do Your Client's Beliefs Play a Role in Meeting Their Needs?

Right now you may be wondering, what causes someone to go about meeting his needs one way, while another person goes about meeting his needs in an entirely different way? That's a good question to ponder.

Could it be that one of the ways someone goes about meeting his needs is determined by his beliefs? After all a belief is just a thought we think over and over again. For example, if I have a thought over and over again about winning an award and making millions of dollars, it's probably because I have a desire to make that kind of money and receive those kinds of accolades.

Where did the desire come from? Desires come in many different ways. You could have grown up seeing your father win awards and make money. You saw how happy it made your father and the relationship he had with your mother. You started to believe that this is the way to a great life. As you saw it more and more from your father, it was in your consciousness as a thought you had over and over and eventually it got engrained in you as a belief. The more you saw it in your dad's life and the success he had as a person, the stronger your belief and your desire grew. You have to have it. You believe this is the key to a successful life. You have a certainty about this way of life.

This may not be a universal truth, but it's true for you because that's what you see. In fact, you made the indirect link between money and awards. You saw how happy it made your father and how happy it made your mom. You believe that for you to be important in life, to be respected and to be loved by your wife, it's all about making money and winning awards. Now, you decide to design your life consciously or unconsciously around "Making Money and Winning Awards" as the secret to life. And why wouldn't you?

Let's examine this further.

- Belief: "Making money and winning awards is the key to a successful personal and professional life." Making money and winning awards is the path you take to fulfilling many of your needs and possibly all your needs.
- Safety: It made your family feel safe when you were a kid. You were always provided for.
- Variety: You were always traveling on vacations, eating out at different restaurants, and meeting different people.
- Relationship: With all that money, dad had all kinds of friends and peers from work. You belonged to all the clubs and mom loved dad so much. Mom loved dad for other reasons but you interpreted it as "Money and Awards."
- Respect: "Money and Awards."

Need I say more?

At a young age, why wouldn't a child adopt those beliefs? If this is all he knows, then this becomes his view of the world. This is how he sees things. This view of the world happens to meet the boy's father's needs at a high level, so why wouldn't the child do the same thing. In many cases the child does.

This child is the hundreds of clients you sit in front of on an annual basis. They are all making decisions based on their view of the world, based on their beliefs. This is how they go about fulfilling their Triple F Needs.

There are other forces in one's personality and identity that shape our decisions, but for now, let's keep it simple with beliefs.

When you ask someone the NQ, "What's life about?" You are asking, "What do you *believe* about life?" Based on what he tells you, you will start to discover what his driving needs are. Needs and beliefs are directly linked to one another. If our needs are WHY we do certain things, then our beliefs are HOW we SEE the world. And how we see the world will determine how we go about meeting our NEEDS.

Right now I could pick up a gun and shoot someone. I do it because this person disrespected me and I want my respect back. I shoot him because I see the world as ugly and mean.

Or,

Right now I could take a hundred dollars out of my pocket and give it to the person on the street corner. I want to contribute to others and giving makes me feel respected and important. I do this because I see the world as a beautiful place and I care for people.

You are starting to see how our beliefs and how our perspective determines a lot about what we will do and why we do it.

If a person sees the world as one big opportunity and everything is possible, then he probably won't be too concerned with living life in a very safe manner. He will value variety over safety and he will make decisions in life based on exploring new possibilities, rather than being dragged into the comfort zone of the same old stuff. What is this person's model for buying? This person buys based on opportunity, variety and growth.

The person who holds back by making decisions based on comfort, probably believes the world is unsafe and there are limited opportunities in this world. What is his model for buying? He buys on guarantees. A lot of variety overwhelms him.

Now you can see how your clients make their decisions by asking a few simple questions. Isn't this great?

"For those who believe, no proof is necessary. For those who don't believe, no proof is possible." - Stuart Chase

Beliefs: Each person goes about fulfilling his needs based on his view of the world, which means, based on his belief systems.

We each go about meeting these needs in a different way because we all see the world differently, and there is more than one way to meet a need.

Part V: Ways We Meet Our Needs

It's my intention here to first give you a couple of examples how people meet their needs. This will prepare you for your client meetings.

Meeting Safety Needs:

<u>Negative Way</u> - Some people go about meeting their safety need by drinking. They reach for the bottle and temporarily feel safe and more comfortable about their problems. People who use negative ways such as alcohol or overeating or drug abuse or procrastination live in denial and fear for their entire lives. When you are safe all the time, you feel unhappy and bored with life.

<u>Positive Way</u> - There is a positive way to go about meeting your safety need. I live my life with a sense of faith that things are going to work out. I can step into any situation with faith and confidence and know that I will always attract the resources and draw from my internal resources within me to make it happen. My faith makes me feel safe regardless of what's going on around me.

Meeting Variety Needs:

<u>Negative Way</u> – On the weekend some people will meet their variety needs by doing drugs. It changes their mental state instantly. They feel different. They know it makes them feel good. This is a way they know works.

Positive Way – Other people go to the beach or a baseball game or a play for variety and a sense of surprise in their life. This is a positive way to meet our variety needs.

How about if you are bored in your job and you decide to leave your job every six months? It brings on variety but it doesn't last. Do you have to leave your job every six months to get variety? No you don't, but that's the way some people do it. This can be very destructive in the long run.

We covered respect, relationship, and life's purpose earlier, so I'm not going to go through them again here.

Activity:

Determine the ways you meet your needs.

1st Fundamental Need: How do you get safety in your life? Make a list now.

2nd Fundamental Need: How do you get variety in your life? Make a list now.

3rd Fundamental Need: How do you get respect in your life? (Money, pets, style/clothing, status, work, etc.)

4th Fundamental Need: How do you get relationship (love, belonging, connection) in your life?

The way you go about meeting your first Four Fundamental Needs will determine whether or not you meet the Fifth and Final Fulfillment Need.

5th Fulfillment Need: How do you get (growth, contribution) purpose in your life?

Now ask yourself, why do you do the things you do? What beliefs are driving you?

Now let's explore how you go about meeting your needs. When you understand yourself, you will understand your clients better.

Question: Why do you and your clients meet these needs in different ways?

Answer: We all have different beliefs and different behaviors we learned over time. Right or wrong, these beliefs and behaviors determine the ways we go about meeting our needs. Drinking and drugs or movies and baseball games! Different beliefs and behaviors, but they are still meeting similar needs for different people. The difference is not our needs, it's the ways we go about fulfilling those needs that make us different.

It's the needs your clients value the most that determine how and what they buy. When you understand your client's needs you will understand what drives them and then you will understand how to present your products and services in the best possible light that inspires them to take action and buy.

Consider this, perhaps your client really wants to buy, but he values safety so much he can't get himself to take a risk. When you become aware of this, you can inspire him to take action. Once you know his driving need, you also know what's holding him back or what will get him to move forward. At times, you will have to really explain the benefits of your product in a manner that helps the client make a shift. The shift could be helping a client see that the benefits outweigh his "Safety Need" of a guarantee. Make sense? Or you could just include guarantees in your product.

Activity:

Let me share the NQ's with you again. Take a moment to answer the questions for yourself. Write your answers down and based on your answers, determine what needs you value the most. Use the NQ's as a reference while I give you some specific client situations that will help bring this lesson home for you.

1) What's the meaning of life to you? Or what's life about?

2) What is the meaning of relationship?

3) What drives you?

4) What gets you out of bed in the morning?

5) What's your passion?

Now, let's talk about WHEN and HOW to use these questions effectively with clients.

Remember what we talked about in the section on Confidence Builders: make sure your process is flexible and conversational. If someone feels like they are being interviewed or challenged, then these questions will not work. They have to come up naturally in the conversation.

Let me reintroduce the tactic I spoke of earlier called STEERING. I am going to demonstrate it in a client process. Then I am going to tie in the NQ's to inspire Sally into action.

Here's the situation:

- You are selling real estate to your customer Sally.
- Sally is a successful entrepreneur.

You ask Sally a great opening question to build rapport: "How did you get started as an entrepreneur sally?"

(Why is this a good question to build rapport? Because every single entrepreneur loves to talk about his business and he will go on for several minutes telling you about it. You are also tapping into Need #3: Respect. Many entrepreneurs have respect as one of their driving needs.)

Sally: My father was an entrepreneur and I decided to take over the family clothing business. I am now the owner with my brothers. Someday I would like my kids to take over the business.

You: Oh, yeah. Tell me about your family, I love kids.

(Here you are discovering how important relationship is as one of her driving needs.)

Sally: My kids are six and eight. They love school and love acting in plays.

(At this point in the conversation you now have some rapport built between you and Sally. Now it will seem natural if you go for a deeper question to really determine her needs. Be conversational! Now is your time to steer her towards the next question.

Steering: You build up the conversation in such a manner that your client is comfortable with you and is wrapped up in the conversation. Now, you want to steer her in the direction that will help you determine her driving needs.)

You: I'm really impressed with your ability to handle all this responsibility and be so successful. I really enjoy learning from people like you. I'm curious, at this point in your life with a successful business and two kids, what's life about for you?

Sally: I love doing what I do and being a role model for my kids. I also want to make sure that my husband and I spend quality time together with the kids to really shape them and give them the best chance to succeed. My father just retired a year ago and now he gets to spend quite a bit of time with the kids.

(Sally is definitely driven by her relationship need.)

You: That's awesome, I love spending time with my family too. I don't have kids yet, but hope to one day. You must be very busy. I imagine life can get hectic at times, what keeps you going every day, Sally? What really drives you?

(You can see how these simple questions allow you to connect with your customer, can't you? It takes the focus off the business when you first meet someone and puts it on developing rapport and a relationship between both of you. Now, when the business conversation takes place, you are both more comfortable talking with one another.)

Now imagine two scenarios:

Scenario 1: Focused on the Property

You take a couple to go see the property; you tell them about all the houses and the neighborhoods; you walk them through the different properties; and then you ask them, "What do you think about this house?" (Notice how the conversation is strictly on the home rather than the clients' desires. You are shooting at a target blindfolded.)

Scenario 2: Focused on the Client

You pick them up and as you show them the properties, you ask them questions as I mentioned above. They tell you about their family, their business, what drives them, what life's about for them. When it comes time to talk about the properties, it is very easy for you tie in all the great things about the house with their needs and their life.

Example: Selling Clothes

Start with basic steering questions. These questions are designed to build rapport and steer the conversation in a direction that makes the following questions natural and conversational.

- What line of work are you in?
- How did you get started in that business?

Now, you ask a question specific to your business such as, "Is there a particular style you like?" (Customer says, "No, not really.")

Now, time for the Needs Question: "I'd like to get a better handle for what style would best suit you, are you feeling like you want a lot of variety, or are you feeling more conservative? Tell me, what's life about for you these days?"

IMPORTANT: I could have just stopped there with variety or conservative. Notice how I asked a needs question that would help me uncover this person's beliefs about her life. I want to truly understand my customers so I can give them the best solution and they are inspired to take action.

All the questions before this one, lead up to this important question.

Here you are finding out about their life. What's new and exciting for them? She may tell you that she just got out of a ten year relationship and she's looking to make some changes in her life. While she may have been conservative in nature before, RIGHT NOW, she is looking for a little variety in her life to spice things up.

IMPORTANT: You always want to find out where they are RIGHT NOW. The needs they value most will change over time, so it's important to focus on what's happening now. Change can happen in an instant. Someone can get a divorce and all of a sudden the things that got him to buy for the last 15 years in relation to his family and his spouse all may have just changed as a result of the divorce. What's life about for them now? Not five years ago or even five seconds ago.

Tip: If you know your profession first and you will know exactly how to tie these questions into your dialogue.

Example:

Let's assume the above customer is an accountant. This accountant had the same job for 25 years, lived in the same town for his entire life and became an accountant right out of college. One more thing, his dad and grandfather were accountants. I'm willing to go out on a limb here and say that chances are his values safety as one of his driving needs.

What would you offer up as a clothing salespreneur?

It makes sense for you to offer him a brand that is timeless, has been around for years and is a good price. Talk about the guarantees. Tell him how thousands of people have been satisfied with the brand, how the clothes last forever and they never go out of style. Are you catching my drift here?

However, if he just quit his job after 25 years and just got a divorce, what might you be thinking?

VARIETY may be the driving need RIGHT NOW. He may want something wild and fun. Feel your client out. Don't assume based on a few questions. A few questions can make you 90% accurate, but dig deeper and build the rapport.

Example:

For the last ten years I have shopped at *Armani.* I love their clothes. They are special, unique and I love going to the stores where the salespreneurs know me. This is very important to me. I also really enjoy going with my friends and picking out clothes for them. I like to know the hottest new stuff that just came out.

What do you think one of my top two needs are?

A good salespreneur would be able to pick up that respect is one of my driving needs. If he is smart, he will make me feel important every step of the way and he will make my friends feel important. When he hears about my business he should know to talk about how I will look in these clothes when I am on stage; how presentable and classy it will make me look. Then he will tell me that I should only have the best because that's what I am teaching my customers as well.

Is this starting to make sense?

By now, bells should be going off in your head. You now have the formula for WHY people buy. The name of this chapter is WHY some clients BUY and others walk. When you use these techniques your clients will never walk again. They will buy because you understand who they are and why they do the things they do. By now, you should understand that the questions I shared with you not only help you understand why your clients do what they do, but it should help you connect with your clients on a deep level.

To inspire someone to take action you must know *what already inspires him to take action.* This could be the most important thing I have shared with you in this lesson. I will repeat it again: To inspire someone to take action you must already know what inspires them to take action.

Part VI: A Product or Presentation That Fulfills All Five Needs

Activity:

Think of your last client meeting. What two needs do you think your client valued the most?

I want you to take a moment and refer back to The Power of Preparation Model in Chapter 2. This model just became even more powerful. One of thc Preparation Habits was to determine how you want your clients to feel in your client meeting. When you know what someone's two driving needs are, then you know exactly how you want him to feel in your meeting. If his two driving needs are respect and safety, then you want your product and you to make him feel important and safe. You can see how powerful this is, can't you?

If his two driving needs are relationship and life's purpose then you want him to feel like he has a strong connection with your product/service and that he is growing as a result of buying your product.

What if your product fulfilled all five of their needs, instead of just their top two? Then there is no way in the world that they could say no.

Imagine this for a moment. You know exactly what your client's two driving needs are that he values the most. The way you discovered this was by asking him the NQ-Needs Questions. At this point you want to gear most of your presentation towards how your product fulfills those two needs. However, let's not forget about the other needs. Wouldn't it be intelligent to craft your presentation around the hypothesis that every product should meet The Triple F Needs of Safety, Variety, Respect, Relationship and Life's Purpose? This is particularly helpful in a presentation to an audience where you have many potential clients.

Everyone knows that Social Media has now become the most powerful communication tool on the planet. It continues to grow faster and faster. What COULD the social media business model and your business have in common?

Right now you may be asking yourself, "What the heck does the social media business model have to do with my business and do I even care?" You should care because anyone who was ever successful was not only creative but he also modeled the success of others. Well, why not model the most powerful communication tool on the planet?

Take *Facebook* for example. Is there something you could learn from their business model and why the average person is on there for 20 minutes a day?

Here is the secret. People are using social media and are on *Facebook* because it fulfills the Five Fundamental and Fulfillment Needs. If you want the secret behind why people buy or why people subscribe to something, here it is:

THE FIVE FUNDAMENTAL AND FULFILLMENT NEEDS

1) Safety: meeting your basic food, shelter and survival needs
2) Variety: Keeping Life Fresh and Exciting
3) Relationship: Love, Belonging
4) Respect: Self-Esteem and Feeling Important
5) LIFE PURPOSE: Fulfilling One's Potential, Contribution to Others

Why we do things, why we buy, why we subscribe has to do with the five needs we have been discussing all along. *Facebook* and other social media sites have mastered the game of fulfilling all five of your needs through their service. And you wonder why people are addicted to these social sites! Anytime an activity consistently meets at least three of our needs, it becomes an addiction.

Now let's talk about getting people positively addicted to your product or service, based on how *Facebook* has done it. Positive addiction sounds like an oxymoron, but you know what I mean; in doing this we must always keep our integrity intact.

<u>Safety</u>

With your products and your business, you must offer someone Safety or guarantees in your product. The guarantee could be your reputation, your service or your product. The majority of people will not buy unless they feel safe to some degree.

Now remember, some people value safety more than others. If you are an entrepreneur Safety is probably not your #1 driving need. If you are someone who has worked for five years in a job that you didn't like, it could be your #1 driving need. Doesn't it make sense to have safety in your offering or product?

How do people get safety on *Facebook*? Wow, get ready for this. You know that regardless of how your day is going or how awful you feel, you can always show up and play on *Facebook*. It's always there. It's the place like the movie Cheers, where "Everyone knows your name," or at least your friends do. And you don't have to talk to someone to connect. If you are phone shy and self-conscious, an easy way to reach out to a sharp businessperson or a friend of the opposite sex is to send him a message. If he isn't interested, there is no verbal rejection and you get to tuck your tail between your legs and quietly move on to the other million people you could be connecting with. It's safe and you are certain what you are going to get.

Variety

Facebook also has tons of Variety. How does *Facebook* fill your Variety needs? From videos, to tags, to articles, to posts, to fan pages to more and more, it is the ultimate variety. You never know who you're going to meet and how many new friends you'll have the next day. No wonder the average user is on for 20 minutes. It takes 20 minutes to figure out how to use all the toys!

Do you think it makes sense to have variety in your product or service? Depending on the client, variety may be a big selling point or not so big, but every product should have it.

Relationship

Clients don't want to buy products from you; they want to have a relationship with you. The beauty of *Facebook* is the power of the ongoing conversation that creates relationships all across the globe. You have love relationships, business relationships, friend relationships and so on. What a genius concept! Do you think it's important for us to learn from and model this model of success? Absolutely.

Even if someone is just buying your product, he wants to feel like he has a relationship with you. What are you doing to ensure that this fundamental relationship need is met?

Respect

Start creating your products so people feel important and respected.

Does *Facebook* make people feel important? Wow! They have a Fan page for people who want to feel ultra important. You can share all the information and videos you want to express yourself and show the world "I Matter." *Facebook* is the Respect Need on a totally new level. Thank goodness to social media for making this self-expression possible.

If you are behind the times and wish that things were what they used to be, then it's time to grow up! We aren't moving backwards; we are moving forwards. So, no matter what your product should find a way to fulfill the first four needs.

And this leads us to the Fifth and Final Fulfillment Need. If you're selling a product and it meets yours and your customers' first four needs, BUT it's not contributing to someone else's growth, it's not good for others, or it's not sustainable, then you will never find your Life's Purpose. You won't be fulfilled and you can't help others become fulfilled.

But, if your product is like *Facebook* and fills the first four needs at a high, sustainable level, the question then becomes: Will your product fulfill the Fifth need? If it does, you will have a customer for life.

Life's Purpose

Life's Purpose is about being in your full potential, being your Best Self. Every day you are contributing and growing. If you're not growing in life, then you're dying. Ask yourself, does your product help people grow? Does your product contribute to the lives of others in a sustainable and positive way? If it does then the sky is the limit for you. If it doesn't YET, then what would that type of product or client experience look like?

On *Facebook* and social media, people love showing up because they grow and contribute to the lives of others by sharing their story or a video. It's said, "What you share, you keep." Every day your Friends list grows and you contribute to the lives of more people. Is this enduring and sustainable? Absolutely. So, if you want to build a successful business or launch a successful product, make sure your product fulfills the Five Fundamental and Fulfillment Needs of your clients.

Activity:

Describe how your product meets each one of your clients' five needs? (If you forgot the definition of these needs, be sure to refer back to the beginning of the chapter.)

1) Safety
2) Variety
3) Respect
4) Relationship
5) Life's Purpose

Since we all have the same five needs, you can be certain that when you frame your presentation in this manner, your sales will go up. Note: Don't tell your client you know it meets their five needs; just make sure your presentation covers it.

What I just shared with you is incredibly valuable. Since you know that every person has five needs that drive him to do the things he does, you also know that your product should hit on these five needs.

Part VII: Meeting Your Own Needs at a High Level

Imagine an area of your life that you absolutely love and have a passion for? Write it down. I'm willing to bet that this area meets at least four out of the five needs.

For example, my business is my passion. I travel around the world teaching others the mindset, skill set and strategies they need to succeed personally and professionally. I am building the most advanced personal and professional growth network in the world. I have an incredible passion to make a lasting difference in your world and in the lives of billions of people. Let's see how this fulfills each of my needs on a scale of 1-10.

<u>Safety</u>: Every morning I wake up and make money doing the very thing that I love to do. My business provides me with the safety, food, shelter that I need at a level 10.

Variety: Every day is different. I'm creating different products, traveling to different places, meeting different people and doing different business. It meets my variety need at a 10.

Respect: I am the CEO of my company. I speak in front of thousands of people. I feel important every single day. I get to solve problems and help people make more money and help them make changes in their lives that they never could have dreamed of. Do you think that fulfills my respect need at a 10? YES!

Relationship: I meet and make friends all over the world. I love my clients, they are my friends. My best friend is also my business partner. I have aspirations of my brother and family being involved in my business. I meet this need at a 10.

Life's Purpose: I teach others how to find their passion and make money doing what they love. I am building a billion dollar company that impacts billions of lives. I am contributing and growing every day in tremendous ways. I love what I do. This need is met at a level 10!!!!!!

Question: Do you think it's easy to sell me something that is going to help my business grow? Do you think it's easy to connect with me if you talk about my business? Absolutely.

This just proves my point earlier. If your presentation explains how your product taps into the five needs of all human beings at a high level, then chances are your clients are much more likely to buy. We just proved it in my example of how my business meets my five needs at a high level.

Activity:

Now refer back to what you wrote down in the earlier exercise about what you love. Does it meet your needs at a high level?

Message: Focus on their top two and go for all five to guarantee the result.

Now, think of something you dislike, such as doing laundry. This meets my needs at a zero in all five areas. You get the point. The things we love meet our needs at a high level. The things we dislike meet them at a low level. And this is the exact reason why we love or hate them: it's all about meeting our needs.

Back to the point I made in the beginning of the chapter. What you desire could be $1,000,000. It could be a new car. It could be a promotion at work. It could be a new dress. We can imagine our desires all day long. Our desires are *wha*t we want. But, in the end *why* we want the million, the dress or the promotion is to fulfill our Five Fundamental and Fulfillment Needs. When you master the Triple F Needs and applying this to your client meetings, your business will go through the roof. You catch my drift.

Activity:

1) Think of the last thing you bought where you acted quickly?

2) What needs did it satisfy for you?

3) Were they your top two needs?

Assignment: This week I want you to meet with five people and use The Triple F Technique to uncover what your relationships' driving needs are.

Chapter 4

Communication that Flat out Sells

"The problem with communication ... is the illusion that it has been accomplished." - George Bernard Shaw

Communication is power. When you learn the strategies and techniques in this chapter, you will be a powerful communicator who inspires others to action so they want to say yes to your phone calls, client appointments and products/services. However, as a salesprenuer using these techniques for selling to or influencing others, make certain your motive fulfills these three requirements:

1) It's inspiring: I call this Class 1 Communication - this is the only communication that should be used to inspire others into action.
2) It intends good for everyone: What you're saying and what you are selling must be the following:
    - It's good for your client/relationship
    - It's good for you
    - It's good in the long term
3) It passes the Integrity Test: Would I do the very thing I am asking someone or inspiring them to take action on?

There are three parts to this chapter:

1) The 14 Secrets Behind The Ultimate Phone Call
2) 11 Communication Tools That Flat Out Sell
3) Setting the Client Appointment 100% of the Time

Let's Get Started!

Part I: The 14 Secrets Behind the Ultimate Phone Call

"I play to win, practice or a real game, and I will not let anything get in the way of me and my competitive enthusiasm to win." - Michael Jordan

Three Warm Up Tips to the Ultimate Phone Call

a) Don't throw up on the person.

Too many times sales people say too much. They throw up all over the client telling him how great their product is. The reason most people do this is because they are nervous, they lack confidence and they are coming from a place of lack. When you don't feel good about who you are you will try to be too much in the presence of others. Instead, be yourself and give potential clients limited information over the phone. People are drawn to the unknown. The mind is always craving more. So feed someone's mind with small bites so they want to know more. If you throw up on them you will only confuse them. Pretend you're talking to a small child who has a limited vocabulary.

I was on a phone call the other day and the person threw up on me. I really enjoyed meeting him by phone and I love his vision, but it wasn't a conversation; it was a throw up session. While I enjoyed listening to him, three to five minutes was plenty of time to hear his story. So, be conscious of the other person's time and his attention span. Its just good manners to not talk for hours about yourself.

b) Don't try too hard.

People who try too hard end up repelling others. I was working with a client the other day and she is the sweetest person in the world and she has an amazing heart. However, no one gets a chance to see her heart because her zeal repels them. She tries so hard because she wants the "sale". So she pours it on, overwhelming the caller with her energy. Remember you want to be in the same vibration as the person you're speaking with. Be calm, be centered and be present with the person. Don't be attached to the outcome of getting the appointment. If you go in with the attitude that it is a privilege for your client to meet you, just as much as it is a privilege for you to meet him, then everything will work out.

c) Get their commitment.

The key to a successful phone call with a potential client is to successfully GET THEIR COMMITMENT for the in-person meeting that you are attempting to schedule.

I want to make an important point right now: Let your potential client know that you know he is very busy.

Let me stop you here. Don't tell them how busy you are, because honestly, they don't care. The worst thing any salespreneur can do is tell people how busy he is. When you say you're too busy, then it seems like this client isn't worth your time. If something is important, you are never too busy.

Most of the time you're not busy and even if you are busy, it's obnoxious and self-centered to say that. You are there for the customer and it's about them, not about you.

The reason you say to your client, "I know you're busy" is because he doesn't know how important what you do is. Let's be clear here. You are calling him. You want his time. I know how valuable what you're offering is, how valuable you think it is and how passionate you are, but your potential client doesn't know that yet.

Let's dive into an example of the ultimate client phone call and you will understand my point more clearly.

Here is a specific example of how it is done. I'm assuming that someone introduced you to the person you are calling. I want to make a critical point here. I want you to get very aggressive about being introduced to new people, even if the person introducing you does not know the other party very well. What I am about to share with you is an incredible process for setting the client appointment every time, even when it is not the strongest referral you have ever gotten. This is an art, so pay attention to every detail.

I am going to teach you how to touch on each of the Five Fundamental and Fulfillment Needs during this phone call. If you connect with all five of someone's needs, it is impossible not to set the appointment.

I'm pointing this out because by now you have learned extensively about the Triple F Needs and I want you to be aware of them every single encounter you have with others. This could be the difference between your getting a client and not getting a client.

Remember our consistent philosophy and belief throughout this book. You are not making a phone call to close this person and just set the appointment. You are calling to see if there is synergy between you. If there is synergy, the natural byproduct will be to set up an opening conversation in person.

The 14 Steps Behind the Ultimate Phone Call

Step 1 - Create the Connection: Relationship and Connection is Fundamental Need # 3.

"Hi John, its Ted McGrath. How are you?"

I ask a question to create a connection right off the bat. The client may say, "Who is this?" but either way you have it covered with the next line.

"Jim Jackson thought that you and I should connect. You know Jim, right?"

Remember, safety is Fundamental Need #1. We have rapport because we know the same person and the person on the other end of the line feels SAFE now because of our mutual connection. Once he feels safe he will open up a bit and share himself with you. This is the start of the relationship. Give him/her an opportunity to speak, even if it's a simple "Yes."

"He's a great guy, isn't he?"

Give your potential client another opportunity to speak. Most people will say more than "Yes." He will say something like, "Yes, I have know him for years," or "Yes, I met him a few months ago," or "Yes, Jim and I just met."

Step 2 - Continue to Build the Rapport.

"I was inspired to call after I spoke with Jim because I really admire your work."

Respect is The Fourth Fundamental Need: all people want to feel important and appreciated. Don't overlook the power of appreciating and respecting others. Find something you admire about the person or something you respect about him and tell him. This builds the connection and makes him feel important.

Step 3 - Find Something in Common.

"Jim told me you're in the Insurance business and I read about you online. I'm an entrepreneur as well."

Remember the last time you had a conversation and you had something in common with the other person? I'm sure you remember feeling connected right away. This makes a huge difference. Make sure you find something in common: a sport, a favorite vacation spot, where you grew up etc., etc.

Step 4 - Tell Him Why You're Calling.

"The reason I am calling is I'm in the XYZ business and Jim thought there would be some synergy between what you and I are doing. I'm not sure where the synergy lies because this is my first chance to get to know you, but are you open to exploring some possibilities?"

Think about it, who isn't open to exploring possibilities?!

Let's assume the person you are calling isn't an entrepreneur. Try this: "The reason I'm calling is I'm in XYZ business and Jim mentioned you are an incredible person to get to know. I'm always looking to meet inspiring people who I can grow with. You never know what will come of it. I'm sure there are some ways that I can help you, are you open to exploring a mutually beneficial relationship?"

Step 5: Diffuse Objections.

Objection 1: What if he says, "No, I'm too busy right now"?

First of all, don't say too much. Be general about what you do. If you're too specific, you may lose him. Be brief and get to the general point you want him to know.

You say, "I understand and that's exactly why I'm calling. I'm sure Jim connected us because he thought we could leverage one another's strengths and collapse time. I do this with all my relationships. I'm sure you have a unique way of running your business and I have some very unique aspects to what I'm doing."

Or you could say, "I know you're busy, that's exactly why I'm calling. I understand how valuable your time is and I wouldn't be calling unless I knew there was incredible potential in us connecting with each other. I've done my research (or, I've heard a lot about you) and I have some unique ideas that could help someone like you."

People like uniqueness. It fills the Second Fundamental Need of Variety.

Step 6 - Tell the Truth.

Objection 2: Do you want to sell me something?

The truth is you don't know what you want from him because you don't know enough about him and you always need to go into the meeting looking for ways you can help. You don't know how you can help until you learn about your potential client.

Here's how I would respond: "Jim, I have no idea what I want from you, if anything. I just like to get to know successful people and I always look for a way to contribute to others."

Or, "Jim, I understand that someone as successful as you probably has people trying to sell him all day long. I wouldn't insult you like that. I'm interested in connecting with people who I can grow with and contribute to. I'm calling because XYZ told me you're all about growing and contributing to others. You're exactly the type of person I would like to develop a relationship with."

The Fifth and Final Fulfillment Need, Life's Purpose, is all about contributing to others and helping them grow. If you live your life helping others grow and contributing to their success, then you will grow and you will be fulfilled. When your client knows you are contributing and trying to help, he will want to meet with you.

Always appeal to a person's desire to grow and contribute. We all have that desire/need inside us. When you appeal to that side, they are off the defensive about you selling them and they are focused on what life is really about.

Step 7 - Potential Questions for Your Potential Client.

You may or may not ask these questions on the phone depending on how much time you have available.

"How did you get started in the Insurance business Jim?" Or, "Tell me a little bit about your business/career."

Never stop building rapport. People always like to talk about their business. Once you hear about his business, find some feature or characteristic that is similar to yours and then tell about your business/career. For example, if he said he has been in business for five years, you might start by saying, "I have been in business for about the same time period as well." When he feels that he is like you, he is more likely to want to meet with you.

Step 8 - Tell Him Briefly What You Do.

It's important to go into your first meeting knowing what he does and his knowing what you do. This way you can both do some thinking before the meeting and you will show up to the meeting feeling more connected, rather than awkward.

Step 9 - Ask for His opinion.

"Jim I am confident that we can truly help one another. I would like to get your opinion and insights on my business and I would like to learn more about yours as well."

I am telling Jim that I want to get his opinion and insights on what I do and I want to learn about his business/profession. The language is very important here. I use this language because I don't ever feel like I am pitching or selling someone. I feel like I am sharing opportunities with him and I truly want his opinion on what I'm doing. At this point I really don't know if Jim is a candidate for my product or service, but I have a pretty good idea that I can help him in one way or another.

Step 10 - Learn about His business/Learn about Him.

Notice above how I told him that I want to learn about his business. When you do meet your potential client, you will do exactly that in the other processes I teach you. You will ask a lot of questions to learn about his business or him personally; and in the end you are going to share about your product/service to get his opinion. Once you learn about him, then you will know how you can help him. Helping him could mean his buying your product or you being a resource in another way that adds value. You won't know how you can help him until you meet with him.

Step 11 - Prescreen Your Appointment.

The pre-screening I do is pretty simple. I follow the Warren Buffet model for hiring and doing business. "Do I like, trust and admire the person?" If you don't, then nothing else matters.

If he came referred to me, I can trust them somewhat. If we connect on the phone, I like him. If I am calling them to meet with him, I better admire something about him.

It's always good to meet a new person and you never know what can come from meeting. He may lead you to your ideal client or he may be your ideal client.

Watch out for people who tell you to qualify people over the phone. I'm assuming that you're not cold calling people here. Those days are over. If you are going to reach out cold to others, do it through the Internet and pay someone to do that for you. Building a business is about doing it with people you like, trust and admire. Those types of people are going to come from other people that you have relationships with. Stay away from a business where you don't want to "sell" to your friends and family. That means you don't believe in the product.

IMPORTANT LESSON: Many sales trainers will tell you to qualify your buyer over the phone. Here is the secret: Results don't come from a ten-step plan or a linear plan. Results come as a result of moving forward towards your goals. If you are just sitting in the office all day and looking for the perfect qualified client, your energy is stagnant and you will be missing out on all the people and opportunities that could "coincidentally" come your way as a result of stepping into a situation. There are no coincidences. Opportunities will show up when you get into action. My advice is step into it. If you were referred to someone and your friend thinks he is a good person to meet, then there isn't much qualifying to do.

"The vast majority of people live lives of quiet desperation."

- Unknown

Don't be quiet; step into it! Success leaves footprints. Be sure to follow them.

Step 12 - Set the Appointment.

"Jim, I'm excited to connect with you. WHEN is a convenient time for us to get together for 30 minutes over coffee?"

I am very assumptive here that we are going to meet so I purposely use the word WHEN. I don't ask him, "Would you like to get together?" This is intentional. Why on earth wouldn't someone want to meet with me when I want to help him or her grow?

Step 13 - Get His Commitment.

I have built enough of a name for myself that I rarely have someone cancel on me. If you have a challenge with people canceling on you, it's important to get their commitment simply by saying, "Jim, I know how busy you are and I know how valuable our time will be together. I just want to make sure that you can commit to this time that we are scheduling. I'm going to be driving across town 30 minutes to see you and I'm very excited to meet you. Are you sure that time will work for you?"

Next time someone considers canceling, he will probably remember that last statement you made and most of the time he will keep the appointment to hold true to his word. No one likes breaking a commitment. People will break an appointment, but not a commitment. Notice that I even use the word "commit" in my statement. Notice also how I said, "how valuable OUR time will be", not "how valuable MY time is." That's obnoxious. Someone recently said to me on the phone that he wanted to make sure it was worth his time. That is a turn off for me.

Step 14 - Send a Reminder.

If you are worried about someone keeping the appointment, send a reminder via your assistant. I used to do this all the time when I was starting out. I still do it at times. If you don't have an assistant, GET ONE! You can't fund growth out of current income. Hire an assistant.

Follow these steps to the ultimate phone call and you will be a master in no time!

Part II: 11 Communication Tools That Flat Out Sell

We all know that communication will make the difference between your being clear on how you can help and your clients being clear on what they want. The tools in this chapter are to be used to reinforce what your client already wants for his life. At this point in the book we haven't gotten into all the processes to uncover your clients dreams and desires. When we do get to these processes you will be able to use these effective and powerful tools to help them build confidence and get inspired to take action on their vision and desires. These tools are not being presented to you so you can get your clients to say "yes" to what you want. They are being presented so you can have clients *reaffirm* what they want. Even when people know what they want, they sometimes have fear or hesitation going after it. Communication has the power to inspire. Use it wisely.

Communication Tool #1: Ask Questions That Elicit a "Yes Response."

YES Varieties: a variety of statements or questions that put the person in an agreeable state, aka a YES state, throughout your conversation.

Have you ever been at a seminar where the speaker comes out and asks you a series of five questions that everyone in the audience says yes to? Have you ever been in a dialogue where someone was trying to prove his point and he asked you questions that you could only say yes to? This is a powerful way to start a presentation or a strong bridge to build into a conversation with someone. Early on in your meeting/presentation you want to get clients to say YES to you.

The questions also break up the monologue and create a dialogue. This also builds rapport, which gets someone to agree with (like) you; agree with your questions; and finally puts them in a state of being more likely to say YES, when you ask them to take action on buying from you.

a) Ask questions that elicit a "Yes Response." Here are some examples that can be used in a presentation to many people or in a one on one conversation:
   - How many people here want to make more money?
   - How many of you want more passion in your life?
   - How many of you want more confidence in your life?
   - You do want more money in your life, don't you?
   - You do want more confidence in your life, don't you?

The majority of people do want the above mentioned qualities in their life and pretty much ALL people will say yes to this. And when they do, here's your follow-up statement: "Great. What I'm going to share with you today will do all of this and much, much, more." This statement confirms that I'm going to give them what they want today.

Activity:

Take time now and create three Yes Questions for your next meeting. Example, if you're selling investments:

- Are you looking to get a higher return on your investments?
- Are you looking to protect your assets?
- You do want a high return on your investments, don't you?
- You do want to protect all your assets, don't you?

Your questions:

1)

2)

3)

b) The Head Nod: a form of silent communication that puts people in a "Yes" state.

Nod your head up and down right now and see what type of response it triggers in your mind. It triggers the word "YES," right? Do you see how your physiology impacts your mind? Try nodding your head up and down right now and say "No." It's really hard isn't it? Now nod your head side to side and say YES. Just as difficult isn't it?

Non verbal communication is very powerful. The simple gesture of the head nod is another YES Variety that will get your clients in the YES state.

Activity:

Next time you see a friend, nod your head up and down, and smile. By nodding your head up and down, it will get him to nod his, and it will trigger the thought of YES.

If you're meeting a client for the first time, try the head nod after you start building rapport with him. Once the rapport is built and you nod your head, watch how he responds.

Example: When doing this with a client, you might say, "Can you imagine how good it's going to feel when you start making $10,000 per month?" (And nod your head up and down while you are saying this.)

<u>A Double Yes Variety:</u>

There is a subtle difference in a double YES Variety. In the above example, I asked a question that they could say yes or no to. In the statement below, I steer them in the direction of saying yes, with the statement/question and I bring it home with a head nod that gets them subconsciously to say YES. It's double the power now.

1) Statement/Question: You can imagine how good it is going to feel when you are making $10,000 per month, can't you? (Client says, "Yes.")
2) Nod your head up and down as you're saying this. (Client says YES again.)

In part a, you are delivering a statement/question they simply agree with. Just the word "imagine" automatically takes their mind into the future to see themselves making the $10,000 a month. In part b, you are following up with a head nod to anchor YES into their physiology. It's extremely powerful when you get a client to imagine a bigger future and agree that this is what he wants for his life. Then it's even more powerful when he involves his physiology by nodding his head and saying "yes." You are helping him believe these things are possible. You bring certainty into his life that he is able to have what he really wants.

c) <u>The Game Changer</u>: small simple plays or ways make a huge difference in getting your clients/relationships into a YES state.

Have you ever wanted someone to take a trip with you or go out to dinner with you? You could tell he was almost ready to say YES and you didn't know what to do?

In life, we all want people to guide us, have our best interest at heart and inspire us to make the right decisions. When you use the processes I'm sharing with you in this series, you will always have the best interest of your relationships and clients at play because you are getting them clear on THEIR desires, not YOURS. Remember, the process of influence is putting other peoples' desires before your own and, in the end, both your desires are met.

Here's a great analogy: Do you play sports or know someone who plays sports? In a football game, it's a matter of inches between your team catching the ball and scoring a touchdown OR the opposing team intercepting the ball and ending the game. Such is life - a game of inches.

Your team is the YES team. You play for them and when you're totally confident, you feel great about making a YES decision for yourself. The opposing team is the No team. You also play for them sometimes. It's the opposing part of you that stops you from making the decisions you intuitively know will change your life for the better. Fear and doubt get in the way.

Now that we have that clear, know that everyone has an OPPOSING team and a YES team. Just like in football when an opposing team is intercepting the ball, your client's opposing thoughts of "I can't do it" are intercepting the ball. The opposing team is the part of their mind that is saying NO, or doubting.

A person of influence always knows how to tap into the YES team when their friend is on the edge about taking a trip, or when their client is on the edge of buying a product that will change their life. Just when you think someone may be hesitating, you want to get them in the YES state and avoid an interception by the opposing team. It's your job to get them back in the YES state and make the touchdown.

Here are some examples of game changers that put your client in a YES state. Notice the format of statement/question: you make an implied statement followed by a short question that gets the client to agree with you. It's as if you are saying, "Look how obvious it is that my product is awesome and it's so obvious that it can help you. YOU CAN SEE THAT!!!!!!" Except you are saying it in a more subtle way.

1) You can see how an investment in this product can help you make a million dollars, can't you?

The client's mind is now off the cost of the product and onto thinking of it as an investment that will make them millions of dollars. Be sure to use the word "investment" instead of "cost."

There were many times in my life when I was hesitant to invest in a program I knew would be great for me. I always had my partner reaffirm that I needed to take a leap of faith and step into it. You are there to help your clients take that leap of faith. They need you to be their eyes at times to see the bigger vision.

2) You can see how this product will make you more confident, can't you?

Assuming the client wants to be more confident, you add the benefit in by using a statement/question that basically inspires him to say YES.

Tip: Always make sure the benefit you add is something you know they want. In the next section I will share with you strategies to elicit what your clients want.

3) "You would love to go on this trip with me, wouldn't you?" Or, "It is going to be an awesome trip, isn't it?"

You can use these statement/question techniques in every part of your life. We all know people who want to do things but need the certainty in their own mind that this is the right decision. A simple YES will inspire them to take the next step. It changes the entire game and will actually change their life for the better. It's the decisions we make in the moments of our lives that shape our future. Help make those moments inspiring and life changing for others.

I hope you also took note of all of the word combinations that I have used with statement/question techniques. For example:

1) would and wouldn't
2) is and isn't
3) can and can't

What if I said, "Can you see how this product will make you more confident?" This gives them an opportunity to say NO and start doubting themselves. We don't want that. This is the power of communication and words that get your client to say YES. I'm not even giving them the room or opportunity to say no. I guide their mind in the direction of YES. Their mind is saying, "Yes, this is what I want." Remember, this comes after they told you what they want for their life. At this point, you have already spent ample time helping them gain clarity on what it is they want.

Here is what we want:

1) I let them know, "You can see," implying YES you can see it!! You can see how this product will make you more confident, can't you?

2) When I use the words "can't you…" I am implying, "Can't you see it?" It's as if I'm saying, "I know you can see it. Can't you see it?"

As a salespreneur, it's your role to make the client feel confident and certain in their decision. At this point, you understand their needs. You know exactly what they want. In spite of people knowing what they want, they still need the reinforcement of other people. You are their reinforcement. These are true Game Changers.

Note: I use this technique at the end of my client meeting when I'm confident that, based on what my client told me, he wants what I have. It's my job to inspire him into action. The right kind of communication has the power to inspire.

d) Word Reverse: reversing the sequence of your words.

Isn't it amazing how this workshop is changing people's lives? Notice "isn't" comes before "is." You still get the client to say YES.

We use Word Reverse because it's important to mix up your YES varieties. If you sound like a broken record, your client will be turned off rather than inspired. When we say the same thing in different ways it reaffirms what that person wants and still keeps it fresh and exciting. It's the same thing when you ask people questions. If they feel like they are being interviewed, they will close off and won't be open with you.

You wouldn't want that, WOULD you?

Activity:

Fill in the blanks as if you were communicating with your client using can, can't; would; wouldn't, is; isn't. Do it and say the statement out loud NOW:

1) You can see how this ________ will _______ can't you?
2) You would like to ________________ wouldn't you?
3) This is the ___________________ isn't it
4) You wouldn't want to____________, would you?

The secret is to get use to hearing yourself verbalize these statements. As we mentioned earlier in our confidence builders, the breakthroughs come in the doing. DO, DO, DO!

Communication Tool #2: Inject Humor into the Conversation/Presentation

Humor helps in the following ways:

1) You get past the client's walls of resistance.
2) It breaks the client's state or mood if they are having a bad day.
3) It gets past the gatekeeper, the logical conscious mind; and taps the subconscious mind, which buys on emotion.

Two powerful tips in a presentation or meeting:

1) Make people laugh, or loosen them up
2) Point out the obvious

When I start my presentations, I say the following, "I started in the insurance business when I was 21. I know some of you are looking at me now and saying, 'He doesn't look a day over 19.'" People always laugh when I say this because it's true. Sometimes truth is funnier than fiction.

I made people laugh and I pointed out the obvious of what they are thinking. Pointing out the obvious is a tension breaker, particularly when you say it with humor. If there is an elephant in the room while you are eating lunch, you aren't just going to pretend it isn't there, are you?

Communication Tool #3: Tension Breaker

Point out the obvious: they obviously know you are going to sell them something or make an offer.

Many times before someone signs up for one of our coaching programs, he gets a free session. I've trained our coaches to say this in the beginning of the call, "At the end of our free session I'm going to offer you an opportunity to go deeper into XYZ program. WHEN you experience this session you will want to go deeper, and IF for some reason you don't want to, that's perfectly okay."

Double Tension Breaker:

Not only did I let him know that I am going to make an offer or "sell" him something, I also let him know it was okay if he doesn't buy.

I rarely use the word "if." I use it here because it is the beginning of the free coaching session. He hasn't experienced the power of my work yet. I don't want him to feel pressured throughout the session.

At this point, the client knows I am upfront about selling him something, and I let him know it's okay if he doesn't move forward. This is important in a situation where you offer someone a gift for free. You have to be clear that you aren't going to push him into something. If the free session was all he needed, then great. This is his decision to make. As a salespreneur I always keep the power in the client's hands. I am never closing him and you should never be closing your clients either. Basically you are telling your clients, "You are here by your own free will and you can leave at any time at your own free will. I simply want to share my gifts with you." Internally you know that they won't want to say no to your gifts and your service because you are that confident in what you do. At the end of the day, a salespreneur helps the client become clear on what he wants and inspires him into action based on what he wants.

Lesson: Notice how I also used the word "when" in that tension breaker above. I am assumptive they will want to work with me and at the same time, I give them an out if for some reason they don't want to work with me. It releases the tension at the beginning of the coaching session and allows them to be present with what we are doing, so they can get the greatest benefit.

Hint: I know they are going to work with me, I'm that confident in what I do.

Communication Tool #4: ConFluence – Cross Between Confidence and Influence

This statement is an example of ConFluence, "WHEN you enroll in my program, you are going to have everything you ever wanted." Notice how I use the word WHEN. I am CONFIDENT using the word WHEN instead of IF. I am CONFIDENT that I will INFLUENCE the person to buy. This is ConFluence. I'm letting the customer know that what I am offering is amazing and I am very sure that he will take action on my offer. I start using the word "when" at the end of my presentation when I understand what the client wants or when I shared amazing information with them and I can see they are inspired by our interaction.

Activity:

Create an example using your product and say it out loud.
WHEN __________________ you are going to __________.

Communication Tool #5: Imagineering: Getting the Client to IMAGINE Already Having the Benefits of your Product.

I wrote earlier in chapter one about the power of being in your full potential or being your best self. When you are your best self you're using both your left and right brain at the same time: the rational (left brain) part of your mind and the creative or imaginative (right brain) part of your mind.

When you use the word "imagine" you get your client to shift from the left brain, where he may be analyzing or trying to make logical sense of why he is sitting with you, to the right brain where he starts imagining. Once someone starts to imagine, he taps into his emotional/unconscious mind. Buying decisions are made from the unconscious mind first. This means that buying decisions are first made from emotion and then backed up by logic. The interesting thing is that once you get someone emotionally vested in your product, he will find his own logical reasons why he should have it. You just need to ask the questions that tap into his logical reasons to support his emotional desire to have what you're offering. The key to getting someone to buy is to have him imagine owning the very thing he wants. The very thing that he wants is not the product. It is the benefit he is going to get from owning the product. Don't talk about the benefits; get him to imagine owning it.

Here are two example statements:

- Imagine what your life will be like, Joe, when you have ten times more confidence?
- Imagine how your family will feel when they see this brand new house that you just bought for them?

Pay attention here and see how I am tying in the client's human needs as well. Suppose I know the need they value most is "Relationship." Not only am I having him imagine a better future, I am also having him imagine a better future with exactly what drives him: his family/relationship.

Even when I am talking about the brand new house that Jim will have, I am still tapping into the emotional benefit of how it will make his family feel and in turn how this will make him feel. I'm tapping into his unconscious mind and then we will work together to find his logical reasons to back up his desire to buy the house.

Communication Tool #6: Pre-Owning it: if all this product did was make you ten times more passionate, it would be worth the $2000, wouldn't it, Joe?

Here the client is justifying in his mind that having ten times more confidence is worth $2000. He starts owning having more confidence because you are getting him to mentally justify it. Once he justifies it in his mind, he pre-owns the product before he pays for it.

By now, you can see how I combine all of the communication tools. I just showed you an example of a Pre-Own Question and a statement/question technique - with "would" and "wouldn't you?"

Communication Tool #7: The Confused Response

Often times in a sales situation or a situation of influence, you ask the person what he is looking for when he hires you as a coach, or a consultant, or as a realtor. What happens if the client doesn't know?

There are two reasons why he gives you a confused response: Either the client really doesn't know because he doesn't know what's available; or, the client doesn't want to commit.

Here is my response: "I KNOW YOU DON'T KNOW. But if you did know what you look for in a coach, what would it be?" Pay attention to two things happening right now:

1) My tone of voice went up (NOTICE THE CAPITAL LETTERS) - the tonality is unassuming and it's also non-threatening. This is important to make the client feel safe and that it's okay for him to answer, even if he's not positive what he's looking for.
2) I use the word "if." "If" signifies that possibly he might know. It doesn't signify that he does know and is not telling me. That's strategic language.

In my experience clients always give me some type of answer when I follow up with the above question.

When you first ask this question you may feel odd because it's a bit outside your comfort zone. That's okay. As my old CEO used to say, "It's my job to make you uncomfortable so that you can be comfortable." Don't worry if your client stops for a moment and looks at you funny; he probably has never been asked this question before.

Communication Tool #8: **Packaging**: presenting the conversation in such a manner that the client is prepared for the information you are about to deliver to him.

Do you know why presenting a wrapped gift is so much fun? The person receiving the gift knows there is something in the box and he's not quite sure what it is. He is in suspense wondering what is about to be shown to him.

I recommend that you always wrap your gifts and package your conversations. When you are about to share a surprise with your client - like he will be investing in a $2,000 program - be sure to wrap the gift. You want him wondering what you are about to say before you say it so he is ready to receive the gift.

Before I ask someone to invest $2000 in one of our programs, I want to make sure that he knows that I made a similar investment myself. Instead of setting him up for sticker shock when he hears the price, I package what I am about to say: "I remember a time when I spent $7500 on my first coaching program. I didn't have any money left to my name. I was frightened, even though I knew this investment was going to return hundreds of thousands of dollars to me. It did and it was the best decision I ever made."

See how I packaged my experience with what the client was about to experience? Since I shared my experience with him, he can now sense what is under the wrapping paper and he's prepared for the $2,000 price tag I'm about to reveal.

Here's something everyone can relate to even though it's not the most pleasant subject. If there were a death in your family, you wouldn't just call your family and say, "Joey is dead." You would package it so that your family member isn't in shock or taken back. You might say, "I want you to sit down and take a few breaths before I tell you this very difficult information. This is really hard for me to say, Joey passed away last night."

Do you have kids? Even if you don't, you have used packaging before. Here is an example we are all familiar with: "Mom and Dad, you are the best parents in the whole wide world." What are you preparing yourself for right now? Your son is about to ask for something he wants and he is warming you up to the idea by complimenting you. Watch how this goes. "Mommy and Daddy, you are the best parents in the whole wide world. Could we go and get some ice cream tonight?"

It's very tempting to say yes isn't it? It's packaged in a nice little love box and the presentation is perfect. You're the best parents, so let's go do the best thing and get ice cream. That's basically what the kid is saying. It's the same as saying, "I spent $7500 on a coaching program; surely you can spend the same amount." Don't you love packaging? You have been doing it your entire life and now I want you to start doing it consciously.

Activity:

Create your own Packaging Conversation before your next client meeting.

Communication Tool #9: **Sales in a Moment**: plant the seed for the moment that's about to come where you complete the sale.

Example statements of Sales in a Moment:

- In a moment, I'm going to ask you to take out your credit card and register for this course.
- In a moment, I'm going to ask you to go to the back of the room and register for my course.
- In a moment, I'm going to get you to fill out the paperwork for your new Mercedes.

Notice how you are telling them the action step they are about to do. You are planting the seeds for what's about to happen and you are giving them a specific action step so they are clear.

If you just tell them to go to the back of the room, you may shock them and break their buying state. If you just tell them to write a check for the Mercedes, they may be rattled out of their buying state. Everything in life has a natural progression and sales should be the same. If you use "Sales in a Moment," you are preparing them for what's about to happen and they are able to visualize themselves doing it before they take the physical action. If you want to inspire your clients to take action, it's important to have them see themselves doing it before they actually do it.

Activity:

Create your own "Sales in a Moment" statement:

In a moment I'm going to ask you to ______________.

Now, tie the word "imagine" into your statement to make it twice as powerful.

In a moment I'm going to have you ____________. Imagine how it is going to feel when you take complete ownership of your future.

Communication Tool #10: Benefits

Clients don't really care about your product as much as they care about the benefits they are going to receive from your product, such as peace of mind, millions of dollars, significance, inspiration, or new skills. The secret is to get them to imagine having those benefits. Benefits can be broken down into two categories:

1) Emotional Benefits: powerful because people buy on emotion. Here are two examples:
   - Jet Blue has a tag line; "We bring you comfort and peace of mind in the sky." When you hear those benefits you can feel the experience that you are going to have with Jet Blue.
   - When you buy this house imagine how happy your family will be. Happiness is an emotional benefit.
2) Tangible Benefits: necessary because people want to know that they are walking away with something tangible. For example:
   - Southwest provides clients with cheap prices and on time arrivals. Their clients know they are going to get a tangible benefit of saving money and saving time when they fly Southwest.
   - Imagine how much wealthier you will be when you buy this house and it appreciates at 6% per year. Making more money is a tangible benefit of buying this house.

Be sure to include both tangible and emotional benefits in your presentation or meeting.

Activity:

List the Tangible and Emotional Benefits of your product right now.

1)

2)

3)

4)

5)

6)

Communication Tool #11: Connecting: connect your client to the benefits of your product.

Follow my example: Let's assume that you are interested in buying my sales course. Here is how I could connect you to the benefits of my product without the product being the focal point. The product is the thing that will get them to the benefits. It's like the bridge that will get them to the island. The benefits are the focal point.

"Imagine how much money you will make by helping your clients achieve their dreams and desires."

Here I demonstrate that I can help you facilitate the dreams of your clients and help you make more money. I have you imagining those benefits instead of imagining a sales course. The sales course is just the process you will go through to get the very things you want.

Now, to connect those benefits to my product, so you associate my product with what you want, I could use this approach:

"Imagine how much money you will make by helping your clients achieve their dreams and desires, when you work with me." (And I point to myself.)

What I'm doing here is connecting their desires and the feeling they get by imagining those desires being fulfilled by working with me. Now they associate me as the person to help them get what they want.

Or, rather than pointing to myself, I could point to a DVD or CD set of my sales course. I don't even have to mention the CD set or the DVD. I can just as easily point to it, and visually they can connect the benefits of what they want, to my product.

In case you're wondering, this technique is called "anchoring." You are pointing to yourself or the product and have them connect the feeling of enjoyment and excitement to the visual representation of the product.

Now it's your turn: Imagine how much __________ you will have when you____________.

Did you notice how I didn't focus on the product? I'm assuming that the client knows what I sell or we have discussed it in one of our prior meetings. I mentioned the benefits of buying the product. I mentioned the benefits of how you will contribute to others. I never focused on the product itself. I pointed to the product so they could make that connection, yet I never had to say anything about it directly. This is a powerful approach.

This is just a different way of doing it. It's not a bad thing if you put some attention on the product and the benefits together. After all, they need to know that they are eventually buying something. This is just an alternative way to get clients to imagine and focus on as many benefits as possible.

EXAMPLE: Let's assume for a moment you are a headhunter and you are hiring consultants.

"Imagine how much happier you will be when you are in a profession that you are passionate about."

Your client knows he is there for a consulting job, so instead of connecting your client to having the consultant job, you connect him to the benefit of feeling more passionate in his profession. Do you see how this works? Now, you try it.

Your turn: Imagine how much __________ you will be when you_____________.

Example: Suppose your client is buying a house. How would you get him inspired to buy the house?

"Imagine how amazing you are going to feel when you are living this incredible new lifestyle."

In this example the client can see himself living this new lifestyle in the house with his family and friends. The fact that he is already in the house you are showing him, makes him connect the feeling and benefits to the product and you don't even have to mention the house.

This is much different than saying: "Imagine how incredible you will feel when you own your new house." When I hear this statement it feels a little flat.

The client WILL have to buy a product that you sell to make that change in his life. We all know that. At the same time, the product is not the focal point, yet it is always indirectly or directly linked to the conversation.

Example: Let's assume your client is buying a car from you.

"Imagine how you are going to feel driving down the highway with the wind blowing through your hair and all the women staring at you." (And you point to the car.)

Try it this way: "Imagine how amazing you are going to feel when you own this car." Doesn't that feel a little flat? It works to a certain extent, yet it never fully gets the client connected to all the amazing benefits of the car

All in all I am just showing you different techniques for inspiring your clients to buy. Rather than talking about your product, you can talk about the benefits and directly or indirectly connect those benefits to your client taking action on your product.

Here is what NOT to do: "I will give you a good price on this product." The reason you shouldn't do this is the moment you start competing on price you are done. The customer's focus shifts from value to price. You want him to see the value in your products and not the price.

Often times customers will come in focused on price and it's your role to get them focused on the value. For example, if I am a customer in that frame of mind, I'm thinking it's going to cost me X for this TV. And once you connect the price to the product, then my mind is saying, "NO DEAL." This is very different from connecting the investment to the benefits of the product. Even so, you want to avoid talking about price upfront, talk about the investment at the end instead. When someone is investing in something, they see it as something that will yield them a benefit in the future. Just remember: *price and product - NO. Investment and benefits - YES.*

If a client asks, "What is the price on this _____?" You would say, "Will you give me a moment to find out, tell me a bit about what you want." Or, "It's $99, (state the price only if you have to) tell me a little bit about what you want."

What if the client says, "I want this model for $99"? You would say, "If you don't mind me asking, what are the reasons you want this model?" Once you understand his reasons, you can understand what benefits he is looking for and introduce him to other options.

Now, try connecting the client's mind to all the benefits of the product. How do you do that? You just did. You got the client to IMAGINE having all the benefits of the product, not the product itself. To continue our example, what good is the TV if you don't get him to imagine watching the TV and how great it will look in his house and all the family members he can have over to watch football? It's not about the TV, it's about the benefits of that TV and how that connects in the mind of your customer. Your job is to help them make the connection. "Imagine how happy you will be when you are watching your new TV in your living room with all your family members over for Sunday football." I connect how the client will feel with the tangible benefits of the products. This is what will get them to buy.

Part III: Setting the Appointment and Creating Lasting Relationships 100% of the Time

Up to this point, I have shared processes to prepare you for your client meetings and processes to inspire your clients into action. However, I also know that it is important to have a powerful process for explaining "WHAT DO YOU DO." Don't people always ask you the infamous question, "What do you do?" Isn't it important for you to respond in a powerful, authentic way and get the END RESULT that you're looking for? And what's the end result? SETTING THE CLIENT APPOINTMENT.

The method I'm about to share with you will easily ensure that you set the appointment. More importantly, it will teach you the art of CREATING LASTING RELATIONSHIPS.

"A customer is the most important visitor on our premises; he is not dependent on us. We are dependent on him. He is not an interruption in our work. He is the purpose of it. He is not an outsider in our business. He is part of it. We are not doing him a favor by serving him. He is doing us a favor by giving us an opportunity to do so." - Mahatma Gandhi

First let's dispose of something outdated and outplayed: prospecting.

What the heck is prospecting? Michael Jordan plays to win and I play to set the appointment and create lasting relationships 100% of the time. There is no such thing as prospecting. Every day and every situation you are in, you are there to set the appointment and create lasting relationships. Are you in it to win it? If you're not, then go prospect. It sounds like a day job that someone hates.

No one likes prospecting because language is powerful. When you use the phrase "creating lasting relationships" your thinking process, who you are and your entire physiology changes, versus using the word "prospecting." It sounds like you are throwing up on someone, so please throw the word away.

When you wake up in the morning and know you are going to create a lasting relationship with someone new today, you feel differently. I just got off the phone an hour ago with a 19 year old kid who was referred to me. We spent 45 minutes together and I wasn't prospecting. I was creating a lasting relationship. I'm going do what I do till the day I die, so when this 19 year old is running the country in 15 years, he will be a pretty good guy to have on my team. I know a special relationship will develop as a result of our authentic and real conversation. By the way, I set the appointment. My appointments are often inviting someone to a conference call or to a free seminar. Turns out his dad may join us on the call. HE's a retired multimillionaire. Never hurts to create lasting relationships.

I was on the phone with another client and her challenge inspired me to write this chapter. She said, "I'm having a challenge communicating what I do to others and getting them interested in sitting down with me." This challenge has always interested me because I just assumed everyone knew you don't ever get people interested in your service, you get them interested in you. And you never get them interested in you until you get interested in them. Here's how you do it.

Do you want to learn the secret to creating a lasting relationship with anyone, anywhere, which will take your life and your business to an entirely new level? Do you want to learn the art of setting the appointment 100% of the time? The two go hand in hand! Are you ready for the formula that will change your business? Here it is:

The Eight Pillars to Setting the Appointment and Creating Lasting Relationships

Pillar 1: Establish Credibility

"Credibilityis like virginity. Once you lose it, you can never get it back."

Imagine you're at a social gathering and someone asks you, "What do you do.?" How can you easily turn this into a conversation that leads to a lasting relationship and a client appointment?

Why not build your credibility in your initial response to the infamous question?

Karen has been in the financial services business for a decade. I told her to respond by saying, "I love what I do. I have been doing it for a decade. I'm in the financial business. Collectively, my partners and I have a hundred years of experience." Right off the bat, Karen builds her credibility.

This is especially relevant in today's economy because people are in and out of their professions. If you've been around for ten years in the same profession, then people feel more comfortable with you. I'm constantly telling people that I have 11 years of experience in sales and influence. It makes a difference. I also refer to my mentor who has 25 years experience in sales and influence.

CREDIBILITY BREEDS CONFIDENCE!

Now you're asking, "What if I don't have any experience?" Borrow someone else's experience.

For example, suppose you're in the software business and you just got hired two months ago. The way you build credibility is by letting people know your mentor has ten years experience or your company has been around for 100 years.

The old saying, "people don't care until they know that you care" is true and provides another dimension to look at. You can care all you want, but if you don't have some type of credibility, you just made a great friend, but no business will come out of it. I want lasting relationships in my life and I want to know that they support my life's purpose. Those are the people I want to be associated with. How about you? Then get credibility.

Activity:

Create your credibility statement now.

Karen's Example: "I love what I do. I have been doing it for a decade. I'm in the financial business. Collectively, my partners and I have a hundred years of experience."

My Example: For the last 11 years I have been an expert in one thing.

To write your credibility statement, remember, these are guidelines. Create a statement that you can own and that gets you excited. Allow your creativity to come out. Write your credibility statement now:

Pillar 2: Make Your "Do" Statement

Once you have built credibility in your opening statement, then you actually make your statement about what you do.

Activity:

Create your "Do" Statement

Karen's "Do" example: "We have developed time tested financial principles that teach families to thrive…"

My "Do" Example: "Teaching professionals and entrepreneurs the mindset, skill set and strategies they need to succeed…"

Your "Do" Example:

Pillar 3: Make It Targeted

What group or niche are you targeting so people can know whether they fit into your profile? If they don't, they can at least introduce you to others. Notice in each of our statements above, Karen and I included the types of people we work with. That's our niche.

Activity:

Karen's Target: Families.

My Target: Professionals and entrepreneurs.

Your Target:

Pillar 4: Make It Relevant

Always make it relevant to what is happening NOW, in today's world, in today's economy.

Activity:

Karen's relevant statement: "We have developed time tested financial principles that teach families to thrive in even the worst economic times…" Karen is letting them know what she does and that her process helps families thrive in bad times like we are experiencing NOW. I'm intrigued with her process.

My Relevant Statement: "Teaching professionals and entrepreneurs the mindset, skill set and strategies they need to succeed in today's economy…" I'm letting people know that they need what I have and they need it NOW in today's economy. It's very relevant.

Your Relevant Statement:

Activity:

Putting it all together in a final statement that encapsulates the first Four Pillars

Karen's Final Statement: "I love what I do. I have been doing it for a decade. I'm in the financial business. Collectively, my partners and I have a hundred years of experience. We have developed time tested financial principles that teach families to thrive in even the worst economic times." Her statement even has passion in it, as she tells people "I love what I do." This is very important.

My Final Statement Example: "For the last 11 years I have been an expert in one thing; teaching professionals and entrepreneurs the mindset, skill set, and strategies they need to succeed in today's economy." My passion comes out when I speak so I don't even have to say that I love what I do. Either say it or be it. They both work well. (Notice that this is my final statement with all the bells and whistles I just explained in the first four pillars.)

Your Final Statement Example:

This is a critical transition point. You have told people what you do in ten seconds. (Anything beyond 15 seconds, they aren't listening.) They know what you do has credibility. They know who you work with. And they know it's relevant. (And you better say it with passion or else get out of this line of work NOW! That is relevant!)

Share your story:

While it is important to say what you do in 15 seconds, there is a way to engage people so they are listening and tuned in to your passion. Stories! People love stories. When you tell a story, you listener goes into a trance. If I were to tell you a story of my childhood and growing up in my house at six years old, you would start to think of your childhood and growing up at six years old. A story takes us to a place so we can experience what is happening. You don't just want your clients to hear what you do; you want them to experience it.

For example, I've been teaching entrepreneurs and professionals the mindset, skill set and strategies they need to succeed for the last 11 years and I remember the day it all changed for me. I was standing on the top floor of the downtown Orlando Suntrust building, staring out my office window. After seven years of success, money and power in the insurance business, I remember vividly being faced with a question that changed my life forever. The question was echoing in my head back and forth like a ping pong ball: Is this all there is? In that moment I realized I wanted to follow my passion and make a true impact in the world. I wanted to be fulfilled and energized about my life. I did the scariest thing of my life that turned out to be the greatest thing ever: I walked out and resigned. I started my own company where I could use my skills, talents and passion to make a difference for others. On that day I started building the most advanced personal and professional growth network in the world. I love my life now.

Did you notice what I just did? I took a rational explanation of helping people with their mindset and skill set and I turned it to real life for the person listening to me. And I did it in less than a minute. Remember, they asked me what it is that I do, so I have the floor for at least a minute. In one minute I engaged their imagination, their senses and their emotions. They can identify with me because they too have asked themselves a similar question. My product is about helping people live more passionately and more fulfilled. I am demonstrating this through my own experience. How can you create your own story to draw your potential clients in?

Activity:

Create your own story now.

Pillar 5: Ask Your Question

He who asks a question is a fool for five minutes; he who does not ask a question remains a fool forever. - Chinese proverb

You have said enough, so it is time to ask your question. Switch the focus and the attention to them so they can feel important and you can develop rapport by letting them speak, which will help them start to feel comfortable with you.

a) Transition Question: So what are you doing these days?

The Transition Question switches the focus from you to them and into having a casual conversation. They are either going to tell you about their life or their career. What else is there? Once you ask the Transition Question, then you pull out one of two steering questions that I shared with you in an earlier session.

b) Two Steering Questions to Ask:

How did you get started in that line of work? (You ask this if they start talking about their career. They will start to tell you their story and the rapport is built.)

Or,

Tell me about your family. (You ask this if they start talking about their family first, perhaps they aren't working.)

Once you find a pivot point to steer them into the next set of questions, you go for it. The pivot point is a point in the conversation where things are flowing so naturally that you can easily ask a deeper question that will help you understand who this person is and why he does what he does. We all want to understand people. This is how we create lasting relationships, right? We create them when we have a deep understanding and liking of the people we care about.

Pillar 6: Determine Their Needs

"Don't ask what the world needs. Ask what makes you come alive and go do it. Because what the world needs is people who have come alive." - Howard Thurman

Let's talk about going deeper with your client using The NQ's - Needs Questions. I shared these earlier:

- What's life about these days?

- What drives you?
- What gets you out of bed in the morning?
- What are relationships about to you?
- What are you passionate about?

After you ask the steering questions, you can then venture into the needs questions. Use any of these questions you want. You will determine what question fits where or if they fit at all.

Perhaps you had a great discussion and you save the needs questions for when you get together in your opening meeting/conversation. Remember, these are tools in your tool kit. A salespreneur chooses what is right at the moment. A process should never be too rigid.

The NQ's will help you pin point what is really driving this person and what inspires him to take action in his life.

Pillar 7: Be Authentic, Ask for Their Insight

Tell them how you feel. "Joe, you are incredibly inspiring and I really respect everything you have shared with me. You're definitely someone who's insight I value. I would like to get your opinion on what I'm doing. One, it may benefit people you know and two, it may even be something you are interested in."

Notice what I did here. I told him how I feel about him. I also let him know I want his opinion about what I'm doing. I don't know if he is a candidate yet and even if he is a fit, so I would like to get his opinion. It's low pressure and it's the truth. You honestly want his opinion.

Once you get his opinion, he may know of some people who would be a fit for it, or he may be interested himself. Quite frankly this is an ingenious and honest approach. Always tell the truth.

Or,

Instead of asking for his opinion on what you do, reverse the tables. "Joe, everything you shared with me is inspiring. I would like to see how I can help you with your vision. I'm sure I know some people whom I can connect you with at the very least."

This approach is a lot smoother because you are asking to help him versus the other way around. Most people like to be helped.

Based on what two needs drive this person the most, I will be able to determine what approach to take. If he values life's purpose and is all about contribution to others, I may take the first approach. If he values respect I would take the second approach.

Pillar 8: Set the appointment

If you didn't go very deep in the conversation you could say, "I really enjoyed hearing about your life; it's quite inspiring. Would you like to connect over coffee next week and see if there is some synergy we can develop?"

Or,

If you learned quite a bit about him and you want to help him with his vision, "Joe, everything you shared with me is inspiring. I would like to see how I can help you with your vision. I'm sure I know some people whom I can connect you with at the very least. When would be a good time for us to connect over coffee next week?"

Or,

If he is really intrigued with your work, you just go for it, "Joe, when can we spend 30 minutes together where I share my process with you? Or, "Joe, take a FREE trial of my product or a sample." Or, "Joe, join one of my free seminars to check this out." Then, "What's your contact info?"

By now you can see that the Eight Pillars to Setting the Appointment and Creating Lasting Relationships is the real deal. They say that life is all about balancing the short term and the long term. In the short term you set the appointment and your questions happened to have set the foundation for a long, lasting relationship. Your client knows you are interested in understanding him at a deep level and that makes for a lasting relationship. Now, that's the result you were looking for, isn't it?

At this point it is time to get into some very powerful processes for face to face, in the trenches, client meetings!!!! This is where we really get serious and focused. You are about to enter the big leagues.

The game has changed today. The processes of old are no longer working. Here is the way I see it. There are several processes that will help you become an expert in mastering *Never Be Closing*. So far, you have only been exposed to a few of these processes.

We already talked about a life changing process for determining your clients' needs. This process is powerful, but it will only take you so far. Let me highlight the other additional processes and then we will explore them for the rest of the book. When you are able to integrate these three processes with one another, you will become a master in sales and influence.

I. **Needs**—Tune into a client's needs and you will make hundred dollar sales all day long. Methodology: Five Fundamental and Fulfillment Needs

II. **Desires**—Elicit your client's desires and you will have thousand dollar customers all day long. Methodology: The Opening Conversation

III. **Vision**—Help your clients crystallize their vision and you will create $10,000 to $100,000 customers who will stay with you for life. Methodology: The Visioning Process

It's time to move on to the final client processes in *Never Be Closing,* and don't forget about the final chapter on "Transforming Objections into Assets."

Chapter 5

The Opening Conversation

"If you greatly desire something, have the guts to stake everything on obtaining it." - Brendan Francis

In this section we tap into your clients'/relationships' desires. Then, in the later sections, you will be taught how to help someone create a clear vision for his life. These processes are your ticket to a six and seven figure income.

Activity:

Make a commitment right now to select five people you want to have a powerful opening conversation with. Who are those five people?

1)

2)

3)

4)

5)

The Opening Conversation

1) This is a simple, but strategic conversation that can be held over a 30 minute cup of coffee.
2) The purpose of this conversation is to determine what your relationship WANTS and to attach his needs and desires to the benefits of your product

3) In this conversation you are not necessarily asking the client to buy your product. Personally, I am not comfortable asking someone to buy when I have not taken the time to understand his situation. During this conversation you are simply finding out what he wants, getting a BETTER handle on his needs, and sharing important information about your service that will inspire him to the next meeting.

Whether clients buy during this opening conversation or not will depend on the type of product/service you are offering. If a client insists on buying, it's okay to let him buy and you should still take him through the remainder of the processes I share in the upcoming sections. This will depend on what you are "selling." It would be a shame to short change your client. You will see what I mean when I share "My Visioning Process" in the next section. Sure you can make a thousand dollar sale right now, but don't walk away from a lifelong relationship that could mean hundreds of thousands of dollars and even millions.

Step 1: Build Rapport

"The most effective way to achieve right relations with any living thing is to look for the best in it and then help that best into the fullest expression." - Allen J. Boone, author, American metaphysics

People do business with people they like, trust and respect. I'm going to share with you some powerful communication tools to get people to instantly like you, trust you and respect you.

a) Creating the Bond with Your Client: Creating the "BWYC".

This is an incredibly important point in building rapport. In fact you are building more than rapport; you are creating a bond with your client.

When you show up to the meeting with your client, who is showing up? Is your Best Self showing up? Many sales people show up to a meeting looking for the deal, looking for the opportunity, or looking for the money. When you show up with that outlook, do you think you will ever form a bond with your customer? Of course you won't. You will be focusing on a thing and not a person.

What kinds of questions would your Best Self ask to build the rapport? Your Best Self would ask several questions to get the conversation to flow naturally.

Let's assume you got referred to your client:

1) "So, how do you know Mary? She's a great person isn't she?

   This is a simple question that instantly unites a commonality that both of you have. Immediately you will feel bonded because you have something in common.

2) "I hear you are in the clothing business. How did you get started in that business?"

   Everyone has a story and people love to share theirs. Even if it's not a great story, people still like to tell it. Always follow the McGrath 90/10 rule. You listen 90% of the time. People love to talk. Give them that opportunity.

3) "You must work long hours in your career, do you have a family? Tell me about your family."

Yes these are basic questions and you still need to ask them. People love to talk about their family or their work. Those two things consume most of our lives. The key here is that you are asking questions that fall within their comfort zone. Remember, people like to operate in their comfort zone. If they aren't in their comfort zone, there is no rapport.

Write this down:

Family + Career + Story = Comfort Zone

You can't go wrong with this formula. Then when you get to questions that they aren't used to being asked, they will answer very naturally and will feel comfortable sharing who they are and what they want with you.

Now imagine you show up as your "Best Self." You are there with all your service, contribution, passion and compassion to connect with your client, to connect with this person in front of you. Your Best Self is now looking at your client's Best Self. Your client can feel that you are showing up in a real and authentic way. You are giving him an opportunity to show up in his fullest expression of who he is. Now, he is being his 'Best Self." Together a bond has been created that is more powerful than the salespreneur and is more powerful than the client. It is the "BWYC." The bond is bigger than both of you. The Bond now has a potential of its own and together you are ready to create in a powerful and meaningful way. This bond is created without words. It is simply who you are being. Be Your Best Self and create The BWYC. When you have a BWYC, you will never be closing, only inspiring clients into action.

b) Compliment the person you're with in a sincere and heartfelt manner.

If someone is wearing a nice jacket, don't just tell him the jacket is nice. Let him know, "The jacket looks great on you." It's not about the jacket, it's about him. The distinction here is "on you." It looks great on *him.*

My friend, Scott, is one of the most sincere people I have met and he always compliments others on their qualities and who they are. People really enjoy that. As long as it is sincere and it comes from the right place, compliment away. If you're not feeling it, don't compliment. Wait till you find something you can appreciate about the other person and then offer a compliment.

c) Find common ground.

There is always something on which any two people can connect. Find out what it is and begin to talk about it. People are influenced by people that they like, trust and admire.

Ask yourself, what do you like about them? Do you trust them? Find something you can admire about them.

Once you listen and learn about their family, career and story, you can easily find a common ground and something to chat about.

d) Mirror them.

Most communication is delivered through your voice and your body, not your words. Words make up less than ten percent of your communication. When you use your voice and body in a similar manner as your client's, you will be more present with one another and you develop a stronger sense of connection and rapport.

Voice:

a) Mirror and match their words.

For example, your client says, "Hey man, you rock! I'm so glad to meet you." (Notice it's casual and cool.) What if you respond in this manner? "It's quite fantastic to meet you also." You are going to lose him. The reason is because your response makes you seem uptight. The initial greeting was very relaxed and friendly. The response was uptight: "quite fantastic." It sounds like you're dressed in a bow tie and your client has his swim shorts on. The two don't match.

b) Mirror and match their volume: If they're loud, speak loudly. If they're soft, speak softly.

c) Mirror and match their pace: If they are speaking quickly, then speak quickly. If you speak slowly they may feel uneasy. When I'm on a call with clients I pay attention to how their pace is making me feel. I like to be very aware of this because it helps me be conscious of how my pace impacts others.

Speak the same words, the same volume and the same pace and you will develop awesome rapport.

Body:

a) Mirror their body stance: Do they cross their arms or touch their chin. Do whatever they do.

b) Mirror their mannerisms: Do they talk with their hands, do they touch a lot. Use your hands and your touch as they do.

c) Mirror their eye contact: Do they stare into your eyes or do they glance away often.

One of my former agents at New York Life used to stare into people's eyes like he was going to pierce them with a knife. Direct eye contact is okay as long as it is soft and not piercing. I actually enjoy looking into people's eyes, but I don't do it in a threatening way. I am also very aware that if the person often looks away from me, I shouldn't look into his eyes as much.

Pace and Lead:

Follow the pace at which they do things and once you match their pace, slowly change your pace and they will begin to follow you. For example, if they talk slowly with low energy, talk slowly with low energy and then gradually change your pace.

Remember, if you can't build rapport with your client, then there is no way he will listen to you and buy what you are offering.

Step 2: Understanding and Identifying

"People will forget what you said, people will forget what you did, but people will never forget how you made them feel." - Bonnie Jean Wasmund

Have you noticed that when someone brings you a situation or a problem, most often he doesn't want a solution right away? That's because you don't have his permission to provide a solution YET. He wants you to understand where he comes from. He wants you to empathize and put yourself in his shoes. Once you do that, he is more likely to listen to your solution or take your advice. Once you connect and understand his situation, then you become ONE with him. Then your advice is welcomed.

It's the same thing in an interaction with a client or someone you meet for the first time. If you walk into someone's office and say, "Hi, I'm Ted and I really think you should change the furniture in your office", the person will think you're a total ass. However if you walk in and say, "Wow, I used to have that same exact desk. I loved that desk. Where did you get it? How do you like it?" You now have something in common. The person likes you and has rapport with you. As you begin to ask him questions, he feels comfortable with you.

Later on in the conversation, after the rapport is built, you could say, "You and I have similar taste. I love the desk you have and I want to share with you the new place where I bought my new furniture. I think you'll like this place." By building that rapport, you are much more likely to get this person to consider changing his furniture, rather than telling him, "You need to change your furniture."

Now apply this to a client situation. If you share with your client that you remember facing challenges in your business; and it was an incredible learning experience; and the thing that changed your business and your life was your willingness to take a risk and bet on your ability to grow and invest in yourself, most likely the client is going to feel connected and identify with you because you understand him. When you ask him to buy your product, he will remember what you shared and he will feel more connected and open to making the purchase.

Step 3: Unfold Their Desires; Tie in Their Needs

"There is one great truth on this planet:

whoever you are, or whatever it is that you do,

when you really WANT something,

it's because that desire originated in the soul of the universe.

It's your mission on earth."

- The Alchemist

a) Question to Unfold Desires: What do you WANT?

I want to share with you the profoundness of this simple question. When you ask someone, "What do you want?" you give him an opportunity to unfold his potential. We all have potential waiting to be unleashed or unfolded. A question gives someone the opportunity to talk what he wants into existence, to share his desires that have been tucked away and to unfold them into existence by speaking about them consciously to another person. Giving someone the space to express and reveal his desires is the most powerful thing you can do. Don't ever forget the "Art of Questioning" that we discussed in Confidence Builder #2.

Remember this: Potential is Powerful. We are all driven by our potential. I know something about this because I am certified in scientific processes that help people unfold their true potential. There is no question more powerful in unfolding potential than, "What do you want?" When you unfold someone's potential, you open his or her life force, desires, confidence, vitality, passion, inspiration, growth and true potential. This is what will help drive him forward into action. We are all driven by our potential. It is a scientific fact. So, use this question:

In a conversational manner ask, "What do you want these days, Jim?"

This is one of the most critical questions in this process. This allows you to truly uncover your relationship's desires. Let him talk. The trick here is to allow him to talk 90% of the conversation (The McGrath Principle). If he gives you short answers, follow up with, "What's important about that?" or, "Tell me more about that."

Example: "I really want to make more money."

1) Echo back the words, "More money, huh?" Echoing back will encourage them to say more.
2) "Yep, seems like we all want more money these days. What's important about that to you?"
3) "More money, huh? Tell me about all the exciting things you will do with more money."

People want permission to talk. These subtle statements and questions will give them the permission they need to open up.

Once you unfold their desires, you want to tie their desires into their needs.

Desires + Needs = ACTION

In the example above, the person wants more money. Once you get him to be specific on the amount of money, you know what he wants. Let's say he wants $1,000,000.

You ask: "What's important about $1,000,000?"

His response: "To live the lifestyle I want for me and my family."

Now, if you didn't dig deep enough, then you still don't know what is really driving him. Is it a lifestyle for him or is it for his family? What is really motivating him? This is why I introduced you to the "Triple F Needs Model." You now have an awareness to dig more and ask better questions.

Your follow up questions are in the next section.

b) <u>Question to Determine Their Driving Needs and How They Make Decisions: What Drives You?</u>

To follow the example above: "What drives you to make the $1,000,000 and live that lifestyle?"

At this point the client will get more specific with you and will reveal what truly drives him to make the decisions they are making.

<u>The One Question "Question":</u>

What's the one question that's been weighing on your mind that if we were to answer together, would make you feel better?

Now you're really getting into the customer's world. You're getting very clear on how you can help him and where he is facing challenges. At this point you know what he wants, what drives him and where he feels challenged. This is a formula for truly inspiring your clients to work with you. I'm sure you can see why you will never be closing again. You don't have to.

Now let's focus on his top two needs. Remember, every person has two needs he values the most.

- If he values relationships be sure to tie in how your product will impact his relationships.
- If he values respect, be sure to tie in how this product will amplify his sense of importance and identity.
- If he values safety, be sure to talk about the guarantees of your product.
- If he values variety, be sure to tie in how your product comes in all different assortments, colors, and varieties.
- If he values Life's Purpose: Growth and Contribution be sure to tie in what this will cost him if he doesn't take action.

Let me share an example that ties desires and needs together:

Desire: To make $1,000,000.
Need: Relationship (he constantly talks about his family).

Your Action Question/Statement: "Joe, the only question that remains is what are the next steps to helping you make $1,000,000 so your family can have the life they have always dreamed of?"

In the above statement I tied in the needs and desires into an Action Question. During this opening conversation, I focus on getting the client to think about solving his challenges and taking action on his desires. I'm not doing a heavy sell at all. I never do a heavy sell. I'm asking questions to develop options for my client. I don't expect Joe to know the next steps, so I will tell him. I will share more examples in Step 4. My next action step may be to set the next meeting.

Activity:

Think of a family member. Now think of the last big decision he or she made. What was driving that decision? Was it Variety, Safety, Relationship, etc.?

This will start to give you clues of how to influence this person in the future.

Step 4: Packaging Their Desires and Their Needs

"Desire is the starting point of all achievement, not a hope, not a wish, but a keen pulsating desire which transcends everything." - Napoleon Hill (American author, 1883-1970)

Have you ever seen a kid's face when you give him a present that he doesn't really like? It's because you didn't take the time to figure out what already inspires him.

"Packaging" is when you bundle needs and desires with the benefits of your product and you wrap it up with a nice little bow and give the exact present a client wants.

It is critical at this point to connect their desires with their needs. To continue our example, if Joe's greatest desire is to make more money because he wants to buy a million dollar house and drive nice cars, then it's pretty likely he values respect. Why talk about all the features of your product when he has given you a narrow window to focus on? Connect his need for respect with his desires for being wealthy and show him how your product will bring him that. For example:

If you're selling real estate and you know the client is in the market for a house, you say this:

"Joe, can you imagine what the people at the office are going to think (if respect is his driving need, he values what others think) when they come over for dinner at your new million dollar home?"

If you're selling investments: (assume the customer's driving need is relationship)

"Joe, can you imagine how your family is going to feel when you have all of your retirement secure and the kids' college education paid for?"

At this point in the opening conversation some clients won't be considering buying your products, and it will be more of a general inquiry into what they want in their lives. That's okay. Don't rush it. The more you learn about them the more you can inspire them.

Important: At this point, you probably haven't given an entire presentation on your products. We are only having coffee in this opening conversation. However, you do understand some of your client's desires and needs and your client has a general idea of what you sell at this point. Your business always comes out in bits and pieces during the conversation. So you can speak about general benefits of your product during this discussion. Your clients are telling you they want their kids' college education paid for and you know your product can do that, so you are driving that home in the above statements. Notice again how we are focused on the benefits of the product and not so much on the product itself. You don't have to say much. You just need to share the three things that your client "must know" in this meeting. Go back to the exercise "The Power of Preparation."

At this point in the conversation you may want to share something with them that you feel they "must know":

I would suggest that the "must know" you share ties into the "one question" on the client's mind.

For example, if the client's one question is, "How do I figure out a way to invest in my future and still pay my bills?" you might share a "Must Know" such as this: "Mary, I know how you are feeling. I just want you to know that 50% of my clients feel the same way and we have been able to get creative enough to find solutions." And you could share a specific story with her to engage her senses.

Once you know what her challenge is, you may set up another meeting to take her through the visioning process that I share in the next chapter. It's your call. You know your process the best.

The key is you're not selling them here. You're just letting them know that you can help them and there are others that you have helped. A "Must Know" is a critical piece of information that you believe will improve your chances of inspiring your client.

Activity:

Pick a relationship or a client that you just had an encounter with and you want to influence.

Do you know what he wants?

Could you guess what his driving needs are?

How would you frame a question or statement to influence him? Try this: "Joe, could you imagine how ________ will be, when you have__________?"

Let's switch gears for a moment. What if your client doesn't really know what he wants? When your client doesn't know what he wants, you have to walk him through "the supermarket."

Example:

When I bought my last Mercedes, I didn't know what I wanted. I'm not a car guy and this was the third Mercedes I was going to buy. So what did the salesmen and my friends do? They walked me through the supermarket. They showed me the whole selection of cars. Once I saw them and knew what was available, I was easily able to weed out the ones that weren't for me and narrow the selection of what I wanted. It came to two cars: the SL500 and the CL500.

You need to show your clients your supermarket when they are unsure or they don't know what they are looking for.

Currently we have three offerings we make to people when they aren't sure:

1) Never Be Closing
2) Creating Change Now
3) Making Money Doing What You Love

My follow up: "If one of these were to interest you, which one would it be?" Very clearly here, I am not assuming anything. I'm just giving the customer a hypothetical; that if perhaps one were to catch his eye or maybe interest him at some point in time, which would it be? This enables me to get to know where he is and what his driving needs are.

At this point in the conversation I would share another "must know." (Notice how I am injecting the "Must Knows" into different parts of the conversation.)

Your "Must Know" at this point could be your supermarket of products or how unique your company is. It's up to you.

Activity:

List your offerings as if you were going to walk someone through the supermarket. (Don't overdo it.)

Step 5: State the Emotional and Functional Benefits

People make buying decisions based on emotion. Be sure to list the emotional benefits of your product.

Emotional Benefits:

Jet Blue: Peace and Comfortability in the Sky

When I bought my first house, the emotional benefit for me was a sense of accomplishment and respect. (Pay attention to my driving needs of Respect and Life's Purpose.) I was 21 at the time. The house was in a highly esteemed area, with "adults" who were my neighbors, so I felt respected and important. It had four bedrooms, so I felt accomplished to have a big house to share with my friends. All of these reasons were emotional reasons for me buying.

One of the functional benefits for buying was that my Real Estate agent said she could knock off a couple thousand if we delayed a few days. What did I say? "Make the deal now. I have a party that I already have planned a few weekends from now!" The point is, the functional benefits of a house were great, but I was more driven to buy because of the emotional benefits so I didn't care about paying more for the house. This is another great example of how emotions supersede logic in the buying process.

Activity:

List the three emotional benefits of your product right now.

1)

2)

3)

Functional Benefits: Functional benefits are more tangible benefits that the client will take away.
Southwest: "Your bags fly free."

Activity:

List the three functional benefits of your product right now.

1)

2)

3)

Another one of your "Must Knows" could be you sharing the benefits of your product. You may not share all of these benefits with your client in the opening conversation, but it is good to have several to choose from when you want to tie them in to the client's needs and desires, as you saw me do earlier.

When you share the benefit, be sure to tell a story about someone who had a similar challenge or desire and this is the benefit he received from working with you. Stories inspire. Because it's an opening conversation, you don't have to directly communicate your product offering. Sometimes indirectly communicating through a story is more powerful.

Step 6: Diffusing Objections.

You never overcome an objection, you diffuse an objection. How? Always understand and empathize with them

Client Objection: Money - "I just don't have the money right now."

Instead of coming up with the solution, co-create one with your customer by asking a question. A question puts the responsibility on them for getting what they want.

"I fully understand, Jim. In fact 90% of my clients are in a similar situation. I also, know that your # 1 objective is XXX. How do you suggest we accomplish this?"

Explore Alternatives: "You know, Jim, my client Jody was in the exact same situation (explain her situation) and here is what she did (offer her solution)."

By giving Jody's solution, you offer an alternative that your client hasn't thought of. And you are indirectly giving him permission to be creative and come up with his own solution or just do what Jody did.

Client Objection: Time - "I just don't have the time."

This is B.S. What they're telling you is that it isn't a priority. If you have determined what your clients want, then you know which need is a priority and which isn't. If you didn't do a good job probing and determining their wants and needs then they can easily use the time objection.

Once we get to The Visioning Process, I will show you how the time objection and any objection can be diffused. We go deeper into diffusing objections in upcoming chapters.

Activity:

Write down a time where you came up with an objection because you just weren't feeling it with a salesperson. For example, I remember my partner and me leaving the Mercedes dealership in Orlando and going to the one down the street to buy not one, but two SL 500's. Why? Because the salesperson offended my driving need – respect.

Two Tips:

a) Expect five no's before a yes.

Most clients may not say "no" five times verbally, but they may be saying no in their head. It's estimated that people will say no an average of five times before they say yes. This is why I share all these processes and techniques with you. I am making sure you address all their no's and turn them into YES. You don't turn no's into yes by forcing a reason on your client. You look for what your client wants and desires, then you help him see past the fear that is preventing him from moving forward. That's what a salespreneur does. "No" will often come up in the client's mind because of fear, or lack of clarity, or avoiding a situation he doesn't want to confront. Your role is to inspire him to confront the challenges and turn the challenges into awesome opportunities. I have devoted an entire section to objections and will show you how to diffuse a client's objections before he ever expresses them verbally to you.

b) Your job is to give your clients permission to get what they want.

Why? Many people have low self-esteem. They won't spend money on themselves or they won't be part of a group they know can help them. It's your role to give them permission to buy and treat themselves to what they deserve. I know so many people who won't spend money on themselves because they feel they don't deserve it.

I'm not one of those people, but you may be, or your friends may be, or your clients may be. They are out there. Be aware.

When you understand someone's driving needs he will always spend money if it fulfills that need. I don't hesitate to spend money on my business because it fulfills all five of my needs.

"Money never made a man happy yet, nor will it. The more a man has, the more he wants. Instead of filling a vacuum, it makes one." - Benjamin Franklin quotes

Step 7: Tell Them What to Do

In the Power of Preparation Exercise from Chapter 2, you already prepared the three things you want them to do. Why is this important? Because your client truly doesn't know your process. You are the expert and he is counting on you to tell him what the next steps are. Always assume he wants to continue. ConFluence!

"Sally, I'm grateful you took the time to meet with me. I enjoyed everything you shared with me. Imagine what your company is going to look like a few months from now. I would be honored to play a role in helping you get there."

Now here are the three things I want Sally to do:

1) "Why don't you spend the next few days and digest everything we spoke about."
2) "In the meantime, I want to invite you to listen in to my next free preview call which will give you great information on how to take your business to the next level."
3) "Finally, let's schedule an appointment for Tuesday where you and I can spend 60 minutes really getting clear on how we can make your business thrive. I have some innovative ideas for you."

Notice what I am doing here:

Reflect - I am giving the client time to reflect on our discussions.

Action - I am giving them an action step to keep them engaged in the process.

Commitment – I get them to commit to scheduling the next meeting.

What if you want them to buy in this meeting?

Reflect - What are your biggest insights from our meeting today?

Action - Tell them what to do.

Commitment - Take the payment.

Many salespeople will just take out the paperwork and assume the client is ready to buy. I believe you should always assume your clients want to do business with you. I also believe that you always need to be aware of what they are thinking. However, I don't believe that you start taking out your paperwork until you have their reflection and thoughts on what they heard and experienced with you. The more they share with you the better. When they share their insights, one of two things will happen:

They share how excited they are and they continue to reinforce in their mind why they made the right decision. This gives the client an opportunity to own their decision and feel great about it. Another advantage when your clients share their insights is it prevents buyer's remorse. If you try to force the sale without finding out where your clients are, later on they may change their mind. Save yourself the headaches and the damage to your relationship. Be authentic, open and transparent throughout the process. NEVER BE CLOSING!

What happens when you get your client's insights and they are unsure about your product? This is fantastic. Now you know exactly where they stand. I will show you how to diffuse their uncertainty and objections in the upcoming section I devoted to it.

Chapter 6

Turning Thousand Dollar Customers into Hundred Thousand Dollar Customers

"Vision is not enough; it must be combined with venture. It is not enough to stare up the steps; we must step up the stairs."
- Vaclav Havel

"Cherish your visions and your dreams, as they are the children of your soul, the blueprints of your ultimate achievements."
- Napoleon Hill

"The Visioning Sales Process"

Simply by reading the name "The Visioning Process" you instantly pick up that this is about helping your clients see their vision. And just as instantly, I can predict the resistance I'll get from sales people:

1) Helping someone with his vision takes too long.
2) I just want to sell this guy my product.
3) I'm not trained to facilitate the creation of a customer's vision.

I fully understand your resistance to this. I felt the same way. And I did it anyway, because I trusted my mentor who had 20 years experience in sales. Let me respond to your concerns.

#1 The Visioning Process saves time; it doesn't cost you time. You're going to have a 45-60 minute conversation with a client anyway. You might as well make it focused and effective, with an end result that makes the client love you, with more money for everyone.

#2 If you just "sell" your product, you are losing millions of dollars over your lifetime. The Visioning Process will make you ten times more money with customers and referrals will flow through the door effortlessly.

#3 Even if you have never facilitated the birth of someone's vision before, there is no time like the present to jump in and learn, despite your fear. It's natural to lack the confidence to implement a new process. With that said, imagine how your results and confidence will skyrocket the moment you make a decision to adopt "The Visioning Process" as a tool for your business. Imagine how this can give clarity to your life. Imagine how it will give clarity to your customers, your friends, your family and your co-workers. It's that good and it's that simple.

By now you're wondering, what the heck is it? Before we dive in, I want to briefly explain how this process came to be part of my life.

When I was 21 years old, I interviewed with New York Life. Now you may know the company is the #1 life insurance company in the country, but at 21 years old, I thought I was interviewing for a magazine. When I walked into the corner office in Orlando, Florida, I had no idea this day and a question I was about to be asked would forever change the course of my life.

This interview was the beginning of a lifetime friendship with Moe Abdou, the managing partner of the firm. I had no idea that I was going to be sitting there for three hours sharing everything about my life and who I was and having the deepest conversation I have ever had in my life. I had no idea that 90 days later I would make $30,000 in one month. I didn't know that I would coach brand new people to make $40,000 in their first month. And I didn't know I was going to help a brand new person make $100,000 off one client, years later. That encounter with Moe Abdou and the question he asked changed my life forever.

"The Visioning Process" is the secret to turning $1,000 clients into $10,000 and $100,000 clients. I have 11 years experience using this process with thousands of clients, sales people and entrepreneurs. It has made me millions of dollars. It has made my partner millions of dollars and I want to share it with you.

In the last chapter I shared the Opening Conversation with you. That process will change your business. The Visioning Process will change your life and the lives of the people you encounter.

Now think about my interview with Moe. When was the last time someone spent three hours to get to know you? For most people the answer is rarely ever. And when I say, "get to know you," I mean really understanding your deepest desires, dreams, ambitions and life's purpose. The majority of life's conversations are often very trivial and inconsequential.

The Visioning Process will allow you to go deep with your clients. In 60 minutes you can achieve a result that has never been achieved before in that person's life. You will help them get a clear vision of every area of their life three years from today; and you will help them get unstuck, get focused and get excellent.

Objectives:

1) Crystallize your client/relationship's vision.
2) Get them unstuck, Get them to Execute, and Get them Exceptional.
3) Client will have strong enough reasons to act and buy your product.

I'm now going to share with you the magic question that changed my life 11 years ago. The Visioning Process is that magical question broken down into seven steps. Some of the steps repeat what you learned in The Opening Conversation, so I will move quickly through those steps.

Step 1: The Visioning Question

"Imagine you and I are having this conversation and its three years into the future, (specify the month, day and year). We're both sitting on an island sipping some margaritas and you're now reminiscing about the last three years of your life journey. As you look back, what must have happened for you to say it has been the most incredible three years of your life?"

First, you want to let the client answer this question in a very general sense. People will tend to be more general before they are specific.

Second, some people won't have any idea how to answer this question and some people won't answer this question at all.

It means one of two things:

1) You need to provide specific categories for them to focus on. I will share more on this in a moment.
2) He or she really doesn't want to have a relationship with you. I strongly encourage you to let the people go who don't want to go deep into this question. If someone won't spend 60 minutes to have a conversation about his life and dreams, then you don't want him as a client.

However, I want to make an important point here. It's YOUR job to get really good at asking this question. If you suck at it, I don't blame someone for not wanting to spend 60 minutes talking with you about it. And the only way you can suck at it is if you don't make it conversational.

Diffusing Resistance:

I remember sitting in my office five years ago with a client who I didn't know. At the time I was in the insurance business. One of my agents brought the client into my office. When I asked this question the client said, "Let's get to the point." My response was, "There is no point. There is only a question. How you choose to answer it will determine whether or not I can help you. Should you choose not to answer it then there is definitely no point in us both being here. That being said, I would be honored to have this conversation with you."

Tips:

1) Practice it with five people who are your friends before speaking with a real client.
2) Make it conversational.
3) Pre-frame the meeting before the client shows up, which means, you probably want to have the Opening Conversation first to tee-up the Visioning Process. If my intention is to set up the first meeting to go right into the Visioning Process, then I let them know beforehand that we WILL need 60 minutes of undisturbed time. "The end result for you Mr. Client is walking away with complete clarity and focus on your Life's Vision and Purpose, would that be worth your time?"
4) In the beginning, be sure to use the template I provide so you can follow and structure the process. Do you remember in the earlier discussion on "Confidence Builders" we talked about having a process? Well, you have arrived. This is the real deal. Now let's rock it!

Back to the Visioning Question:

Once you ask the Question, there are three categories you want them to focus on. Let me reiterate the question again. I want you to imagine you are asking your client this question and then focusing him on the following four categories:

1) Personal
2) Professional/Financial
3) Fun/Entertainment
4) Contribution

The Visioning Question: "Imagine you and I are three years into the future. Now imagine you are reminiscing about your journey over the last three years. What must have happened over that period for you to feel like it has been the most incredible time of your life?"

Initially you will get a general answer to a general question. As a professional salespreneur, it's your role to focus your client on each specific category, so that you are clear on what is most important to your client and so he is clear as well. Remember, most people do not know what they want. You will be the most valuable person in their life when you help them unfold their potential desires.

Here are example questions of how to move the client through the specific categories:

First: "I appreciate your openness, Joe. Let's get a bit more focused here. Tell me, what must happen personally over the next three years?"

Next: "Your personal vision is inspiring, Joe. Tell me about your professional dreams as you imagine yourself three years into the future."

Next: "I'm very clear on your personal and professional goals, Joe. Tell me what you want to do for fun. It can't be all work and no play."

Last: "That's exciting Joe. How about the contribution you want to make to others. I know that our driving need and what really fulfills us is contributing to the lives of others. What do you want to do in that area of your life?"

By now, you have captured your client's three-year vision. He couldn't have done it without you. I use three years because it's far enough away to be considered a Vision, yet close enough to feel real and possible to your client.

At the same time, what good is a vision if you can't see five feet in front of you? It's time to focus on what must be done NOW to realize your future vision. I call this the S.E.E zone. It's kind of like the end zone in football. When you get into the end zone you put points on the board so you can win the game. Well, when you get into the S.E.E. zone, you add points to areas of your life to get you closer and closer to your vision.

Step 2: S.E.E. (Stuck, Execute, Exceptional)

a) Stuck: Where are you STUCK?

"Joe, you have an amazing vision. I also know that with an incredible vision there are challenges and areas of life where we are stuck. Where are you stuck?"

To start, help your client get unstuck in one area of his life. Once you become an expert in this process, you can consider helping him in two areas.

b) What is one area of your life that you MUST EXECUTE ON?

We all have areas of our lives that if we WERE TO EXECUTE BETTER, every other area would flourish and thrive. The area could be finances, health, relationships, projects we're working on, etc.

c) What are you good at that you want to be the EXCEPTIONAL at?

Or you can rephrase the question this way: We all have areas of our life we are good in. What's an area you are good at that you want to be EXCEPTIONAL at?

Here, I am helping my client dig into his passion. We tend to want to be EXCEPTIONAL in areas that we have passion in. It's not enough to be great anymore. We have to be EXCEPTIONAL!

Follow-up questions to help the client take ownership:

- Can you imagine what your life would be like when you are no longer stuck in that area?
- Can you imagine how great you're going to feel when you EXECUTE ON ____?
- Can you imagine the results you will get when you are EXCEPTIONAL AT ______?

I like these questions because they get the client out of the present problem and into the future, OR they get the client focused on the results/benefits rather than the task at hand.

Step 3: What's Important and Why it's Important?

WHAT: Gives us a Vision for our lives

WHY: Gives us a Purpose for our lives

I heard this in a movie recently, "There is a purpose behind all things. I trust it's so."

Example: "Joe, now that you have this amazing three year vision for your life personally, professionally and financially, fun-wise and the contribution you want to make, tell me…"

a) "…what's most important for you personally?"

You must know his #1 goal in each area. This way, when you offer a solution at the end, you are feeding back the information based on THE most important thing to him.

"That's awesome. I can see how that is really important. I'm curious…"

b) "…why is that most important to you?"

- Tonality is very important here. It's not a strong WHY; it's a soft why.
- The WHY is the fuel for action; it's the purpose behind all things.

Let me demonstrate why this is so powerful and important. On June 30, 2005, I knew I had lost the ambition for my career at New York Life. I was seriously ready to resign and find something else to do. Oh yeah, I was making great money. The best money I ever made in my life up to that point. But I just didn't feel fulfilled. Remember, my two driving needs are respect and life's purpose.

However, in one day, I was given a big enough reason WHY this job was important to me and everything changed. The turning point was when my company offered me a promotion opportunity of a lifetime. I saw the opportunity for growth and I turned on a dime and went out and personally did $120,000 in commissions in 30 days. Mind you, I wasn't even in personal production at the time. The promotion opportunity made me feel respected and proud and I was inspired to add $120,000 of commissions to the millions of dollars in production our office would do that month. WHY? I had a strong WHY!!!!

When people discover why a goal is important to them, they will feel empowered and energized to accomplish it!

For example, let's move to the Professional/Financial category.

If I (the client) told you these three things are important to me:

1) I want to do $1,000,000 in commissions this month;
2) I want to get promoted to Senior Partner; and
3) I want to have the corner office.

You would ask: "Ted, out of all those incredible professional and financial goals, what is most important to you?"

My response would be: "b) Getting promoted to Senior Partner." As the facilitator and salespreneur, mark and star that answer as most important to your client professionally or financially.

You should follow up with, "Ted, I'm so excited for you. WHY is the promotion so important to you?"

And I would say, "I want to feel accomplished. I want to impact millions of lives. I want the respect of my peers. I want to make a lasting difference in the company." This is my fuel for action.

Now, you know exactly WHAT I want and WHY I want it. You have given me a strong reason to take action as a client. In the end, when you are proposing a solution, there can be no objections on my part for you to diffuse. If I ever did object, you just feed back one of my most important professional goals and my reason for wanting that. What excuse could I give you?

If there is still hesitation, there is a deeper issue, which is normally about money. Remember, someone who wants something bad enough will be resourceful as long as he takes ownership of what he wants. In an earlier chapter, I shared with you the language and processes to help clients take ownership and move into taking action.

Hint: Later when you are about to offer your product to me, do you think it would make sense to tie into your presentation how you are going to help me get promoted and make a lasting difference in the world? YOU BETTER if you want me as a client.

Now I know what you are thinking: "I can't do this; the process is too long. I'm not good at asking questions. I have never done this before." I understand how you feel and I'm telling you that everything you are thinking is an excuse. We are talking about being the Michael Jordan of Sales. This is going to take practice and dedication. When you master this, it will become second nature and you will find yourself using these questions all the time. Trust me, after 11 years of asking this question thousands of times, I KNOW!

Let's assume you are a car salesmen or a real estate agent: Would it be smart, in a very conversational manner, to learn about my company and ask about my goals in the next few years? When you get good at these techniques you can use them in any situation.

I used to use them on a first date. My dates had no idea that I was using a process because I became the process. I share this to explain to you how simple and casual the conversation can be.

Right now you still might be thinking, "I could never use this process in my business." That is not true. Go back to the Confidence Builders chapter. Do you remember what I said about making this flexible and conversational? Once you know the process, you will find yourself intuitively using it in all your conversations to the point where it becomes completely natural.

Let's get back to the Process:

IMPORTANT: For each of the following categories, you want to ask these questions:

- What's most important to you?
- Why is that important to you?
  1) Personally
  2) Professionally/Financially
  3) Fun/Entertainment
  4) Contribution

The Goals that are most important to your client will be used at the end of your presentation to come up with a solution strategy and to inspire him into action. It's simple. You already have one "most important" goal in each category and the reason why that goal is most important. Those are the four most important goals in your conversation. Then you will figure out which one is THE MOST important out of the four Most Important Goals.

VERY IMPORTANT: "Out of all your goals and desires Mr. Client, if you had to pick one, which one would be most important? Next most important? And last most important?" (Be sure to feed back the goals your client shared with you throughout your discussion.)

This is critical. When you are offering a solution at the end, be sure that you start with what's most important, then second, then third etc., etc. This is how your client's brain is processing the information. If you mix up the sequence, you may lose them.

Step 4: Strategy for Implementation

All along you may have been wondering, "When is Ted going to get to the point where he shows me how to make a sale?" What you don't realize is that you are making the sale in this conversation and you don't even know it. When people have CLARITY, decisions are EASY!

What I'm about to share with you really has nothing to do with "making a sale" even though it will result in your client buying your product. All you have to do now is give your client a STRATEGY for implementation. You are the facilitator of your clients' dreams and they are in charge of taking charge of their life. Take what's most important to them and package it in a framework that gives them complete clarity and a direction to take action in. As long as you present their most important goals in order and you tie in how your product can help them accomplish this, THEY WILL BE INSPIRED TO TAKE ACTION.

Influence: Inspiring others into action by knowing what already inspires them.

Have you ever seen the TV series from years ago "All in the Family?" The old guy, Archie; used to look at his wife or his son-in-law and say, "What the hell is she talking about?" This whole time when you heard my definition of influence you were probably wondering, "What the hell is Ted talking about?" Well, NOW you know.

Your client has just given you the answers of what inspires them in life and to inspire him to take action NOW, you must show him how you can help him reach his #1 goal. When you do that, he will be inspired to ACT.

Strategies:

1) Get Them Unstuck
2) Get Them to Execute
3) Get Them Exceptional

Example of a client situation:

1) <u>What is most important</u>: #1 Goal is to make $1,000,000 next year
2) <u>Why $1,000,000 is important</u>: To give his children everything he never had and to send them to private school.
3) <u>Where the client is STUCK</u>: He has no money - $2,000 in bank account - and is lacking confidence.
4) <u>What he wants to EXECUTE on</u>: Building a consulting business.

5) What he wants to be EXCEPTIONAL at: Being a great leader and manager of people.

Strategy 1: Get Unstuck

Many times clients aren't really stuck. They are just emotionally drained and need a big enough reason to go forward. They need someone who can inspire them with a strategy and a clear path to get there. Most of the time the solution is as simple as the language you use and the picture you paint for them. When people are clear, they move forward. When people are stuck, they don't move. Watch my language and watch how simple this can be.

a) "Joe, you want to make a million dollars in your business this year, I understand the economy is bad, money is tight and I realize you only have $2,000 left in your bank account. If I could help solve your money challenge and get you on track to your $1,000,000 goal, would you be interested in working together? I have been there and I know you will breakthrough this challenge right away."

   I am reiterating his most important goal - $1,000,000. I show him I understand his world and I'm empathizing with him. Hypothetically, I'm solving his problem and getting his feedback by asking a question. It's always great to know what your customer is thinking and feeling. These are called Feeling Questions. I will talk more about these in the next chapter.

b) "We've gotten to know each other very well over the last several days of working together and I know how much it means to you to make the $1,000,000 and send the kids to private school and to make sure that they can spend time with their friends. In fact, you mentioned that this was the most important thing for you, your kids."

   I'm reiterating his most important goal and reiterating WHY it's important, (which is to send the kids to private school). I'm feeding back his goals so he can see me as a mirror reflecting them back to him. This further validates his goals and the decision in his mind for wanting what he says he wants. This gets him that much closer to buying my product.

c) "Joe, Is there anything more important to you than making the $1,000,000 for you and your kids?"

I am feeding back his most important goal to him to get him to agree that this is what he said and what he still wants. I am confirming this is what is most important to him. This way there is no room for error on my part to start interpreting what I believe to be important. Keep your values out of this. It's about the client.

d) "I am so confident that WHEN you INVEST in my program "Mastering Sales and Influence" you are going to make your investment back immediately and you are going to be able to make the income that sends your kids to private school. IMAGINE how your kids are going to FEEL when this happens?"

Here I'm using the skills learned in the section "Communication that Sells":

1) Always use the word INVEST. Never use the word "cost."
2) WHEN means that you are confident you will influence them to buy (ConFluence).
3) IMAGINE he is able to see and visualize his kids in private school.
4) FEEL he is tapped into the emotional reason of WHY he should buy.

Important: Throughout the Visioning Process I constantly share the three things my customer must know about my program (see Chapter 2). It's your job to continuously bring those three things up about your product throughout the process. I also had you create powerful stories to share about others who have purchased your program. At this point in the process, your client knows what you do and what you sell. He may not know the specifics but he has the general idea to a point where he knows this is something he is interested in. When you talk to him about investing in your program as you just did, it is very natural and it flows because you have weaved it into the process over the last several meetings or over the last 60 minutes of conversation.

Critically Important: As we proceed here you're learning communication tools and techniques to integrate into your presentation of your product/service. You know your presentation the best, so it's time to create your best presentation by integrating all the tools I have shared with you throughout this book.

Go back to Chapter 3 and be sure that your product/service covers all five of the human needs and touches on the two that are most important to your client. When your presentation hits his top needs, he will do everything in his power to get it.

The only thing that would stop someone from getting the very thing he wants is fear and a lack of clarity. However, when someone is clear, his fear starts to fade away because his vision gives him faith that things will work out. When people can see the future, it's not as scary as when they are totally confused. In my own business, when I am not clear, I get stressed and fearful. As a result I don't take action. Money is never the real issue, its fear and lack of clarity. Get them clear and the fear will start to fade away. Get them a vision and they will find a way to pay for what you have, as long as it fits within their vision.

This is the most important point in this entire chapter. This is what the visioning process does. It gives someone clarity and confidence of what is possible in his life and you become a part of the support structure to help him get there. Without you, he is toast. The greatest CEO's in the world need someone like you and so does every person you encounter. That's how powerful this process is. I don't care if you don't see how this fits into your current sales process. It is a must for you to find a way to innovate your process and include the power of the Visioning Process.

Does every person on the planet feel stuck at times?

Does every person on the planet want to execute better?

Does every person on the planet want to be exceptional (even though they won't admit it)?

As Wesley Snipes said in his old movie "Passenger 57," "You damn skippy" this means yes, yes and yes.

Let's continue and let's get Jim completely Unstuck.

e) "Imagine how your life will change Jim, when you have____ (fill in the benefits)."

Here you want to share the need/benefit that is going to be fulfilled for Jim.

In our live program "Mastering Sales and Influence," I share the functional and emotional benefits. Here is an example of benefits to our program:

<u>Functional Benefits</u>: An incredible skill set in sales; an instant increase in your income; greater confidence in client meetings; more structure to your sales process; a deep understanding of what makes people take action; more free time to spend with your family; more money and a greater lifestyle.

<u>Emotional Benefits</u>: Greater passion in your work; greater confidence in your abilities; more passionate and energizing relationships; a happier and stress free life; a peacefulness about your future.

Activity:

Make a list of all the emotional and functional benefits of your product. Think of how you would tie your benefits into your conversation with Jim. Do it now.

f) Action Statements: Getting the client in the mindset for action.

<u>First Action Statement:</u> "You can see how 'Mastering Sales and Influence' will bring a sense of peace about your future for you and your kids, can't you, Jim?"

Here I'm still building on the things you learned in the section on "Communication That Sells":

a) I'm tying in a Yes Variety statement that get's the client in a YES state.
b) I am tying in an emotional benefit in this statement - "sense of peace."

Second Action Statement: "Once you take this course you will easily be able to increase your income by ten times, won't you, Jim?"

a) Another YES variety by using the words WILL and WON'T.
b) I tied in a Functional Benefit of increasing his income.

Third Action Statement: "In the program I teach you how to tap into your client's driving needs in 2-3 minutes and you are going to love it. Can you imagine how much more passionate and energizing your client relationships will be?"

Pay attention to all the techniques I just used from "Communication That Sells":

a) Sales in a Moment: I am going to teach you (planting the seed of the value I will add).
b) Sales in a Moment: You are going to love it (planting an emotional seed of the benefit he will receive).
c) Imagineering: Can you imagine (he is imagining a bigger future).
d) Emotional benefit: Passionate and energizing relationships.

Important: I understand that Jim only has $2,000 in his bank account and I also know that the reason he only has that is because he is not taking the action he needs to take. I'm not taking responsibility for his money situation. That is his job, not mine. I am inspiring him to make the best decision for himself right now. I know the decision is to invest in my program because I know he will make it back. When people have skin in the game and a lot on the line, they will take action. My role is to MIRROR Jim's desires and his vision. If a man or woman can't get excited with a clear vision and strong reasons then I don't know what will excite them. I am using my techniques, processes and skills of influence to get Jim to see HIS bigger future. When I do he will become resourceful and do what he needs to do to invest.

Can you remember the last time you wanted something badly enough? You did everything in your power to get it, didn't you? Make your clients want it badly enough and they will make it happen. You can't push them into action. You can only influence them to see what their heart has always wanted.

Strategy 2: Execute

What area of Jim's life must he focus on in order to Execute?

Anybody who is successful knows that Execution leads to results. When you can get your client to focus on one area that can make a difference in his life, THAT ONE AREA will make all the difference.

Execution area: Building his consulting company to assist in achieving his $1,000,000 goal.

You may be thinking, "What if Jim brings something up that I can't directly help him with?" or, "What if I can't provide a service that will fulfill that ONE area for him?"

It's good for you to be thinking this, because this is what makes you a salespreneur rather than a salesperson. A salespreneur will take ownership of the situation and be a resource above and beyond what any salesperson would be. You are going to bring in your team of friends, resources and associates and make sure you are the bridge to helping your clients achieve their goals and desires. In doing this, you will build your brand and your uniqueness in the market place. Clients will pay a premium to do business with a salespreneur. This is why I say that "The Visioning Process" will bring you clients worth $100,000 to you. That's the caliber of process you bring to the table and those are the caliber of people attracted to you. Once you start BEING the person who helps your client get clear on their VISION, your whole life and business will evolve in ways you never imagined.

Think about it this way. If you help Jim Execute on what's most important to him, he will be more likely to buy your product or service. The clearer he is and the more inspired he is, the more he will see value in doing business with you.

A salesperson only sees the part, and that is the whole picture for him.

A salespreneur sees the WHOLE and realizes how he can play his part.

It's your job to see the big picture and to be the resource that your clients deserve.

Let's assume that what Jim needs to focus on is something you can help him with. Suppose your product can help him build his consulting business. At this point you now have even more confirmation from Jim that he truly needs and wants what you have.

Let me demonstrate: "Jim, not only will we solve your money challenges; we will also be able to help you with your consulting business as well. Our platinum package will help you get unstuck and it will help you focus on your consulting business. If we were able to assist you in both these areas and I was able to discount your investment today, is this something you would be interested in?"

Note that I am not asking him to buy yet. I am just giving him a hypothetical "Feeling Question," so I can get a feel for where he is.

"Great, Jim. We will work out a plan that is doable for you in a bit."

It's time to go deeper into the process with Jim before we inspire him to write the check and buy. Stay with me. Let's proceed with getting Jim into a buying state of mind.

Here are a few subconscious triggers that will get Jim in the buying mode. Have you ever watched a preview for a movie that you wanted to see? If you see the preview once, you are excited to go. If you see the preview several times in that day, you are even more motivated to go and it is very likely that you will. That's because your mind is being triggered every time it hears or sees the preview.

At this point in the conversation, you want to get your client in the BUYING mode. This is your opportunity to create another preview for your client. Throughout the process we have been allowing Jim to preview the movie. Your client is pre-viewing what the future will be like every time you paint a new section of the picture. Let us continue to paint your masterpiece.

Buying Statements: Communication that triggers the desire for the client to BUY and act on his #1 goal.

Notice how we use the word "buy" in this example. When a client hears the word BUY, even if it is in a different context, they are still hearing the word BUY. This is exactly what you want them to do.

Examples:

"By (BUY) now Jim, you can see how "Mastering Sales and Influence" is going to make you more money in your business." (#1 Goal)

"By (BUY) now you can see that with all this money, you can hire some great people to help you build your consulting business and market your business." (# 1 Focus)

Now that I have my client inspired to buy and hearing the word BUY, let's switch gears to continuing to add value to them as a salespreneur.

Shifting Question: The purpose of a shifting question is to move the focus from your products/services to another area that will help your client move forward with his Vision. (If your product does it all then stay focused on your product. With that said, in my experience, most products don't fit all the clients' desires and goals.)

Here I shift the focus off my product to other resources for Jim: "Jim, would you be open to having me introduce you to some of my peers who specialize in marketing and getting your brand out there?"

Pay Attention:

a) At this point I have shifted from being someone who just offers a product to someone who is going to be a resource to help Jim get what he wants.
b) Notice the language of using the word By, BY (buy, buy) to get his mind unconsciously focused on buying my product while I introduce him to my peers who can help him take his business to the next level.

Here I am doing an excellent job of focusing his subconscious mind on my product and his conscious mind on what he needs/wants to EXECUTE on.

At this point I'm stacking on the value. I'm not asking him to buy my product first and then I solve his other challenges. I'm proposing all the ways I can help him and then I'm clear with him about the next steps for my product/service.

Strategy 3: Best

What is Jim good at that he wants to be EXCEPTIONAL at?

Everyone wants to be exceptional in some area of his or her life. We all want to live out our BEST SELF. Imagine the difference this will make in your business when you help others become their BEST SELF. Jim wants to be the EXCEPTIONAL at leading and managing others.

Example:

"Jim, I have some great tools I am going to share with you to help you become a better leader as we work together. There are two tools that have helped me tremendously over the years in building my companies: 'Now Discover Your Strengths' and 'The Kolbe Index'." (I'm adding value here with products and tools that aren't mine.)

"Both these tools will help you manage and lead others in an incredible way." (This is what he wants to be excellent at.)

"When we work together, Jim, I am excited to introduce you to my peers who can help you grow your organization. I am going to bring you these two books and profiles as a gift. I'm excited for you to start our 'Mastering Sales and Influence Program' on (XYZ date)."

Tips:

- Notice how assumptive and confident I am that he is going to work with me.
- He will get to meet my peers when he decides to work with me.
- He will receive these tools and gifts when he works with me.

"I am going to throw in a bonus coaching session for you as well, Jim." (I continue increasing the value by giving him a coaching session with me which he already knows works. That provides certainty in his mind that he knows he will get more value.)

Tip: Always throw in a bonus. It increases the value and the perceived value.

At this point in the conversation, how certain am I that Jim wants to work with me? About 99%.

The only thing that could get in the way is his challenge of money. So it's important for me to address this before I tell him the investment he is going to make for the course.

Step 5: Consistently, Consistently, Consistently Feed Back Their Strategy

This is one of the most important Steps in the entire book that you must learn and drill into your mind. You must consistently feed back your client's strategy. This is an absolute must.

Their strategy is what you have been helping them develop throughout the entire process. What will keep them engaged is hearing their strategy being fed back to them. People stay engaged when the conversation is about them or what interests them. The biggest mistake sales people make is talking about how great their product is or talking about all the product benefits when they have no idea what the client's strategy is. The client's strategy consists of getting them unstuck, getting them to execute and getting them to be exceptional. This strategy is tied into their most important goals. As a salespreneur you must consistently feed their strategy back to them.

I was on a phone call to buy a company's product because I knew it will help us as an organization. Not once did the sales person try to uncover my desire and even when I told her, she never fed it back to me. Do you know how frustrating this is as a client?

Think of all the clients who may be ready to buy and they don't because you weren't able to elicit their strategy or you weren't able to feed back a strategy that connected with them.

Strategy Musts:

- Strategy Must #1: Use a thorough process such as the Visioning Process to elicit their strategy.
- Strategy Must # 2: Feed back their strategy exactly how they shared it with you.

When you do these two Musts, you will have 100% of your clients do business with you.

Time to Feed Back Jim's Strategy: "Jim thanks for your openness and sharing your vision with me. I admire everything that you want to accomplish and it would be a privilege to play a role in helping your vision become a reality. Here's what I have gathered from our discussion today. Your most important goal is to make $1,000,000 this year to give your kids and your family everything they have dreamed of. With that $1,000,000 goal in mind Jim, my job is to get you unstuck, get you to execute and to assist you on your path to being exceptional. Here's how we are going to do it:

(Stuck) "I understand that you may feel stuck with $2,000 in savings. By now, you know not to worry because the way we get you unstuck is to immediately help you get a return on your investment with XYZ Product. You will see results instantly.

(Execute) "I am also going to help you Execute on building your consulting business by introducing you to my peers who are excellent in this category. Once you start bringing in the money by working with me, they will give you a great discount on their services because you're being referred by me.

(Exceptional) "Lastly, I am going to send an email to you today to give you the links to those two programs that will help you become a better leader. They have nothing to do with our company, they have helped me over the years and I want to share them with you.

(Important) "The only question that remains is how long it will be until you are living this amazing vision that you have painted today?"

Notice how I just inserted another Feeling Question. I'm not asking him to buy yet. I'm putting out my feelers to see where he is and to see if there are any last minute hesitations to handle.

Most of the time, if you have presented a product or service of value and you have been thorough in your presentation; the only hesitation for the client will be time or money. We addressed the money challenge with Jim already.

Let's look at two different scenarios:

1) Let's assume that your client is feeling good and he is 95% ready to buy. You can sense it. Always be prepared to throw in bonuses and discount your product if at all possible. There is a certain way to frame this to get your

client 100% ready to buy with no hesitation. If you know your client is feeling good, move on to STEP 7 where I show you how to wrap up the meeting and inspire your client to buy. (Note: Even if you don't face any objections, you will still want to study and learn Step 6: Diffusing Objections. In fact, I have an entire section devoted to this below.)

2) Suppose your client's hesitations didn't come up in the conversation and are now coming up towards the end of the meeting. Or perhaps your client never verbally expresses his hesitation and you still sense that there is something holding them back. Let's move on to Step 6.

Step 6: Diffusing Objections - Turning Objections into Assets

Two biggest Objections:

1) Time

2) Money

The key to this section is that you never have to overcome an objection. I call it "Diffusing Objections," because with my technique, you will diffuse the objections before the client ever brings them up. This step presents some methodologies to diffuse an objection before it's even presented. If you see an objection as an asset to get your client closer to having what they want, then you will welcome objections and know that you are almost to the finish line.

We both know that the client is thinking about money, so diffuse that objection in advance. You can actually address the money objection before they bring it up. This is the best way to address all possible objections. Diffuse it before it comes up.

If for some reason the client brings up the objection before you are able to diffuse it, then this is how you handle all objections.

This is the Golden Rule: You always empathize and you always understand.

"I completely understand Jim, I have been there before. AND I agree with you that money is tight right now, I see it with all my customers."

Now, Diffuse the Objection with:

1) A story.
2) A Statement - in Step 7 you learn how to make a statement with bonuses and discounts.
3) A Question - I have a whole section devoted on diffusing objections with questions.

Diffusing Objections with Stories:

Jim is "stuck" on having only $2000 in his bank account. Here I tell him a story that indirectly gives him a solution that he is able to do this and to be resourceful. People relate to stories. It taps into the emotional part of their mind.

Storytelling:

a) I remember my meeting with Jody two years ago. She didn't have the money or the time to take this course. She was rushing home one night after her day job of working as a marketing contractor for *Taco Bell*. When she got home she had to feed four hungry children. Her friend, Susan had told her to get on one of my teleconferences. She just didn't have the time and still something was telling her she had to get on that call. She did and when it came time to make the investment in the course, she really didn't have the expendable money to do it. But, she Stepped Into It and signed up that night. Jody's entire Life Purpose has been to be a coach. Did you know that last week I wrote her a check because now she is coaching my clients? Our system works Jim and I know you are going to get to your $1,000,000 goal and we will look back at this day and smile."

   Jim is relating at this point. Like Jody, he doesn't have the expendable money but he wants to make money as a result of this course, like Jody is. I'm also sharing proof of someone who has gotten results from my program.

b) "One of my clients called the other day to tell me she already started making money because of one of the bonus tools I shared with her. I hadn't even given her the main product yet and she was having financial success as a result of our bonus tool! I am going to give you that bonus today Jim. That is over $100 in value."

Take Away: The take away is designed to get the client to realize their hopes and dreams could be taken away in a moment and they better act NOW. Tomorrow is promised to no one.

In the "Take Away," I share a story of someone who missed out on an opportunity because he wasn't willing to invest in himself.

"I remember the day we invited Michael Ray to come teach a course in our office called 'Creativity in Business.' We paid him $60,000 to come and work with 15 of our agents. All the agents had been there for less than a year and we asked them to write a $3000 check to invest in themselves and their future. That was a big investment and it paid off because in the next 90 days we had the best results of our life.

"There was one guy, John, out of the 15 others, who decided not to invest in the program. He had all the talent, he had all the potential and he didn't do it. I believe that decision altered his life in a way he will never know. The point is if, he "Stepped Into It," he would have been opened up to a world of personal potential he never knew existed. It would have paid him many times over, but he passed it up. Every day when he walked by the room to see us in our course, I sensed that he knew he passed up the opportunity of a lifetime.

"I understand where you're coming from, Jim. I have been there before and I know that you don't want to miss out on this opportunity. To make you 100% confident in your decision today, I am going to throw in a bonus and give you a discount."

Activity:

The Objection Diffuser: Write down ten possible objections that your clients could have about your product. Write them all down. Create a story or use a technique to diffuse each objection.

1)
2)
3)
4)
5)
6)
7)
8)
9)
10)

Objection: "I don't have the time."

"Jim, if this course were FREE would you enroll in it today?"

Clients normally say yes to this and that takes the time objection out of the equation. Time is an excuse, especially when you know what their #1 goal is and you have already fed back their strategy in the order of what is most important to them.

"Although this course isn't going to be FREE, I'm sure you understand the value you often get out of something is in direct proportion to what you actually invest into something."

Or,

"Jim, your #1 goal is XYZ, correct? Since this is your #1 goal and my program is going to help you accomplish that, it would make sense to make time for what's most important, wouldn't it?"

The client has nowhere to go because you know too much. It's natural for them to squeal and squirm when it comes to decision time. Most people don't like to make decisions without someone's approval.

They truly need you to inspire them and they need your confidence to override their fear. CONFLUENCE!

This is my direct approach to diffusing the objection by using the information the client has shared with you. In the next chapter I give you the exact verbiage and steps to diffuse any objection. Please don't use it like a robot. Learn it, understand it and incorporate it into your style and personality. Nothing is written in stone. It's been proven to work for many professionals and the best salespreneurs actually adapt the process so it fits their style. When I say follow the process, I mean follow it but use your senses to adapt it when necessary.

Objection: "I just don't have the excess money."

"I fully understand, Jim. Ten years ago when I was asked to invest $7,500 that I didn't have, my mentor said something to me that I never forgot: 'You can't fund growth out of current income.' I never forgot that. That decision to stretch myself and find the money truly changed my entire life."

These were some simple way to diffuse objections before they come up or when they come up. In the next chapter, I will share a step by step formula to handle all objections.

Even though the objection is diffused, it's now time to get your client to ACT.

Step 7: The Final Countdown

I call this the Final Countdown because you are literally seconds away from having a brand new client whose dreams are about to unfold.

If your client has no objections and the process is flowing, you jump from Step 5 to step 7. If your client has objections and you handle them like I did with Jim in Step 6, then it's time to integrate your communication process.

a) <u>Let's integrate Diffusing Objections with The Final Countdown:</u>

Remember the end of my conversation in Step 6 where I was diffusing Jim's objection to not having the money: "I fully understand Jim. Ten years ago when I was asked to invest $7500 that I didn't have, my mentor said something to me that I never forgot, 'You can't fund growth out of current income.' I never forgot that.

That decision to stretch myself and find the money truly changed my entire life."

b) Now I add the Retail Investment:

"The retail INVESTMENT for my program is $997, Jim. That's not the price you're going to pay. In a moment I'm going to offer you a discount WHEN you register today."

It's the final countdown and we are close. I want to reassure Jim every step of the way that he is making the right decision.

"You know, if all this course did was make you ten times more income, it would be worth $997 investment, wouldn't it? Don't worry though, I understand your money challenges and I am going to discount your investment."

c) And then I add a Bonus Offer:

"Jim, I'm excited to work with you and I know you want to move forward on this. I'm also going to throw in the bonus coaching session, which is over $250 of free value. And I'm going to discount the retail investment. If I were able to do that, would that make your decision easier to move forward?"

Notice that I'm always asking questions to find out where my client is. I never assume they are ready to go until I get their verbal feedback. When I get their verbal feedback, I study their body language as well.

d) Actual Investment:

"When you register today Jim, I will discount your investment to $847 and I will throw in a free coaching session for $250 in value. I will do ALL of this for only $847. Does this feel right for you, Jim?"

Again, I am checking in with how my client is feeling. They can feel if it is right for them. I want to avoid buyer's remorse or refunds in all possible scenarios. Don't leave anything on the table.

e) Get His Commitment:

"Are you committed to doing this today, Jim?"

I always like to get someone's commitment. A commitment is stronger than a simple, "Yes."

Sometimes people will hesitate and want to think about it, even though it feels right and they know they want to do it. As human beings we have problems with commitment at times. This is natural.

"Jim, I'm offering the discount and the bonus today. I don't know if they will be available in the future. Chances are they may not. Imagine what this is going to do for your family and your life. You are making the right decision. Are you committed?"

"Will it be check or charge?" or "Great, I will need your credit card to take payment today."

> **Tip:** Always give the client a reason to take action TODAY. It doesn't always have to be a price reduction. It could be a bonus you throw in.

f) Avoid Buyer's Remorse:

"You are going to love this program, Jim. You made an awesome decision, I promise you."

There's nothing worse than when someone regrets a decision they made, even if it was a good decision. Always make sure that you let them know they made a great decision. Human nature makes us need validation from others. You don't have to thank them for the sale, just congratulate them on their decision and let them know how excited you are for them. Thanking them for the sale implies they did you a favor. It is a mutually beneficial relationship. Congratulate them on their decision to invest in your product and let them know how grateful you are to have gotten to know them.

Now let's dive into Diffusing Objections at a deeper level, in Chapter 7.

Chapter 7

Transforming Objections into Assets

When you learn to transform a client's objections, you will become a master in facilitating an effective and efficient client meeting. Part of what causes meetings to be ineffective is not knowing what your customers are thinking. In this chapter, you will learn how to discover what they are thinking and to use their thinking as an asset. You will learn how to use their thinking to your advantage and diffuse any hesitations or objections before they come up. After you learn to diffuse an objection, you will learn how to turn it into an asset that inspires your client into action. Sounds powerful, doesn't it? Let's find out just how powerful you can be! And remember, never be closing. Never overcome an objection, diffuse it. Never close a client, inspire him into action!

Spend Less Time, Make More Money

The Process Accelerator: As long as you are effectively using the time with your clients, it's okay to spend less time with them. Time is the one thing we can't get back and that makes it one of our most valuable assets. When you're effective with your time, it will be because you understand where your clients are in the buying process. Sales people often waste time presenting irrelevant information because they don't know what their clients are feeling or thinking. By learning where your clients are, you accelerate the buying process. Now, your clients are happy because you were conscious of their time and feelings and you make more money.

Here are three reasons why you make more money.

1) You gain a client instead of losing him by saying too much. Less is more.
2) When you know how they are feeling/thinking, you can activate those feelings to get them to take action.
3) You will have more time to see other clients because you have more time in the day.

Now it's time for your client to buy.

Action Questions: When your client is ready to buy, there are basic action questions that you need to ask. An Action Question implies, "Let's do this. It's time to buy."

Examples:

1) Do you want the bronze package or the gold package?
2) Will it be cash or charge?
3) Are you committed to move forward?

These three questions are assumptive and I use them when I sense the client is ready to buy. However, before you ask your client to buy, you must influence him first. Part of being successful in influencing clients is having the skill set to transform their objections into assets. To transform an objection, you must first understand your clients' view of the situation.

Definition of Influence: Inspiring your clients to take action by understanding what already inspires them.

I shared this definition with you earlier and showed you several processes, such as the Triple F Needs, to understand what inspires your clients. Influencing others is what you do as a salespreneur.

Suppose for a moment that your client has some objections about your product or service. Suppose he is moving away from buying, rather than towards buying. Let me introduce you to a technique that I call Diffluence: diffuse a client's objections and influence him into action.

Definition of Diffluence: Diffuse + Influence.

One of the biggest mistakes sales people make is waiting until the end of the process before they diffuse the client's objections. You should be diffusing objections throughout the entire process. In order to diffuse an objection, you must know where your clients are in the buying process. Let me introduce you to a technique called "Feeling Questions."

Feeling Questions: The purpose of these questions is to feel out the client. You want to find out their level of interest in your product. You are not asking them to buy. You want to use feeling questions throughout your time with a client to find out your client's buying temperature.

Feeling Questions to ask yourself so you remain conscious of your clients' temperature:

- Are they ready to buy?
- Are they neutral?
- Are they clueless about what you do?

A Feeling Question for your client is designed to discover where your client is in the buying process and to get your client to say "Yes" to your product in a hypothetical manner.

Feeling Questions to ask your client:

- Are you with me?
- Does this make sense?
- What are you thinking?
- How do you feel about that?

I will ask a client these questions during my conversation or presentation in order to create a dialogue. As I learn where he is and how he is feeling, I adjust my presentation to make sure I am on course to reach OUR destination. Our destination is the client buying. Does this make sense?

At this point, your client may bring up an objection and this gives you an opportunity to diffuse it or to give them more clarity/information if this is what they need.

Three Feeling Questions:

a) Opening Feeling Question (use at the beginning of meeting): Are you thinking about buying a car (a house, a jacket, an investment, etc.) TODAY?

I would only use this question if I were selling real estate, cars, clothes, etc. these are more straight forward, tangible products. If you have a variety of products and services it may be difficult to ask that question without getting clarity first. You make the call. And I would only ask it after you have spent the time to build rapport with your client. An opening question doesn't mean it's the first question you ask; let's be clear with that. When you've built the rapport and you feel it's the right time to feel the client out, you ask the question. It's an "opening feeling question" on the opening or first question.

By asking this question, you find out upfront if the client is considering making a purchase, neutral or clueless. If he says, "No," you can still influence him. He isn't saying he won't buy. He's just saying he isn't thinking about it right now. Once you know where he stands, you know what direction to go in. Think about it, if someone is ready to buy, don't waste time giving him information he doesn't need. If someone is clueless, you need to spend the time giving some basic information about your product.

b) Middle Feeling Question (use in the middle of meeting)

The Middle Feeling Question is asked to discover your client's challenge or where he is stuck. This may be an objection that he will bring up at the end. Wouldn't it make sense to handle that challenge in the middle of your presentation?

Suppose, for example, his challenge is having a limited amount of cash flow to invest. Ask, "In order to make $100,000 this year, wouldn't it be worth a $2,000 investment on your part?"

You trade the challenge with the benefit your product or service will bring him. You help him to say, "Yes."

You try it: In order to have ________, wouldn't it be worth ___________?

Suppose Time is his challenge.

"Wouldn't it be worth six weeks of your time to have your most important goal of accomplishing XYZ?"

You help him say, "Yes" in advance by framing this question in relation to his most important goal. If he says, "No" that's great also. You get to find out where he is and what he's REALLY looking for.

You try it: Wouldn't it be worth __________ to have ____________?

Follow-up Question: "I'm curious, hypothetically, what would make XYZ service worth your time?"

Now, he will tell you what he is looking for in his ideal world. This gives you more information to use to influence him and give him what he wants.

c) Final Feeling Questions (use at end of presentation)

1) "If we were to get you unstuck in your finances, you would most likely move forward with this, wouldn't you?" (I'm implying that the client is close to moving forward, that's why I use this at the end of the presentation.)

2) "Does this seem like something you would be interested in?"

Remember, I'm not DIRECTLY asking him to move forward. I am using a "feeling question" to find out his level interest. If he tells me "No," he's not giving a definite "No" because I'm not asking an "Action Question" yet.

Notice the difference between: "Are you committed?" or, "Are you ready to move forward?" and "Does this seem like something you would be interested in?" It's the difference between a client giving a definite answer and the client giving an answer of possibility: "Yes, it's possible I might be interested in your product."

These Feeling Questions will help you accelerate your client process. They can be used throughout your presentation to discover where your clients are and to gather information that can help you solidify the buying relationship. Before, we were anticipating possible objections that COULD come up. Now, we are handling actual objections that DO come up.

The Art of Transforming Objections into Assets

a) Embrace the objection. If you start arguing with your client, you have lost. You will not win this argument. When you embrace the objection, you accept it rather than resist it. You take the negative energy away by accepting it. Now you have an opportunity to transform it into something positive. It then becomes an asset for you to use to inspire your client into action, rather than repelling your client from taking action.

b) Reflect their words. If the objection is, "It's too much money," then reflect the words back, "Too much money, huh?" In most cases, they will now tell you why they think it is too much money. Reflecting their words allows them to hear what they are saying. This prompts most people to expound upon their original response and share more about why they have this objection.

After they fully explain the first objection and their reason, elicit other objections.

c) Elicit other objections. "I will definitely address your first challenge of 'it's too much money' in a moment. Before I do that, are there any other challenges you have with the product? I want to be very thorough here and answer all your questions." If they tell you this is their only challenge, you know that once you solve it, they will be ready to buy. If they have another challenge, address it one challenge at a time.

If the client shares their objections and echoing their objection back doesn't prompt them to give you more information, use this approach:

d) Ask a Question. Make sure you ask this question with humility and great respect for the other person. "I understand that money can be a challenge at times. Would it be okay if I asked you, what would make you think our product costs too much?" The client will tell you his logic behind why it costs too much. You will now understand where he is and what he is thinking. This is very important.

e) Put it to Bed. "Hypothetically, if we were able to solve that challenge (or, challenges), would you be interested in moving forward?" You have put the objection to rest by indirectly letting the client know you could solve his challenge. Most likely he will say yes to this. He told you these were his only objections/challenges, so there is nothing else for him to say.

Activity:

What are the most common objections that come up about your product?

Practice using the five previous steps in diffusing these objections.

Let's be more thorough and go deeper on diffusing objections.

f) Understand and Appreciate. Don't fight the objection. Understand and appreciate where your client is coming from. You can find a way to appreciate how they're feeling, especially since you understand their Triple F Needs and they have shared personal information with you. If you argue with your client, you are done. You are letting your ego get in the way.

Let's continue with the COST objection.

Example: "I understand how you feel about the price. It is a big investment."

When you use these words, you agree with your client and let him know you recognize how he's feeling. You put him at ease and help him be open to your suggestions.

g) Substitute BUT with AND. Take note of my language: "I understand how you are feeling. It is a big investment and…" If you use BUT, you completely ignore and discount his objection. When you use AND, you accept the responsibility to co-create a solution with the client. You team up to resolve the challenge, rather than fight against your client. One word makes all the difference.

h) Transform the "COST" Objection. "I understand your challenge with the cost. It's a big investment and here's what I'm wondering…"

   1) …wouldn't it make sense for us to figure out a strategy to find the money?
   2) …wouldn't the benefit of having this product be much greater than the investment you put into it?
   3) …what if we were able to get you the benefits immediately and come up with a strategy for getting the money?

Notice the techniques combined:

- I understand the challenge;
- I used the word AND;
- Then I ask a question.

Rather than focusing on the problem, I have transformed the problem into an opportunity to move forward. A question redirects the focus from the problem of price to a solution. We transform the objection by asking a question.

When I worked with New York Life, my agents would have excuses about why they weren't getting their client appointments.

Rather than get sucked into the problem, I would ask a question leading them to figure out the possible solution, "I understand what you are going through. I used to face this challenge all the time and wouldn't it make sense for us to figure out a solution for your clients to keep their appointments? What might that solution be?" We already know what the problem is, so a new question focuses the attention in a new direction. If I provide the solution, they have no ownership over it. If I ask a question, I give them an opportunity to accept and embrace the question. Then I continue to follow up with other questions.

i) Feed back their desires. "I understand that it's a big investment. Other people have told me this and, I'm wondering (insert their desires and ask a question)…"

   1) …you just told me your # 1 goal is this. If we could get you the results to meet that goal, wouldn't it be worth the investment?

   2) …you just told me that you want to make more money. This program is going to help you make more money. Isn't that the exact reason why you should take our program, so you are never in this position again?

   3) …since I know you want your family to have an incredible life, isn't it true that your family's lifestyle is more valuable than $2,000?

   4) (Rationalize it) The investment in this program works out to ten cents a day if you use the product for the next five years. You would agree that it's worth ten cents per day in return for making hundreds of thousands of dollars over five years, wouldn't you?

Now you try it: I understand that it's a big investment, other people have told me this and, I'm wondering:

   1) …you just told me your #1 Goal is _____________ . If we could get you the results to meet that goal, wouldn't it be worth _____________

   2) …you just told me that you want _______________. Isn't that the exact reason why you should take our program, so you are never in this position again?

3) … since I know you want________, isn't it true that _______is more valuable, then __________ (fill in price of your product)?

4) Rationalize it: The investment in this program works out to ____ per day, if you are using the product for the next ____ years. You would agree that it's worth _____ per day in return for ______________ (fill in benefit) over __ years, wouldn't you?

Bringing it all together:

- I understand
- I agree that it's a big investment. Others have told me this
- Transition with the word AND, not BUT
- I'm wondering
- Ask a question to transform/diffuse the objection
- Feedback their desires

The Final Countdown. Act as if the client is ready to buy. You have diffused all the objections. There is no reason why they wouldn't move forward at this point. Act as if they are ready to buy without acting forceful or pushy. You are in the final seconds of having a brand new customer; be confident and be ready to influence. It's the Final Countdown!!

I believe price should never prevent anyone from having what he wants. There is always a way. At this point in your meeting, you may have shared the price of your product or you may not. I never discuss price until the end. Also, remember to us the word INVESTMENT instead of PRICE. At this point it is time to address the investment in your program and to get your client to take action NOW. This is what you train for as a salespreneur. It's all on the line, your client's future and your success. Are you an influencer? Are you able to put your client's desires before your own and in the end both of your desires are met? I know you are able and I know you are ready. Let's do it!

I shared a specific example of this process in the last chapter. Let's walk through the steps again:

a) Retail Investment:

"The retail investment for my program is ________. That's not the investment you are going to make WHEN you sign up today. In a moment I'm going to offer you a discount."

"You know if all this course did was made you ten times more income it would be worth a _____ investment, wouldn't it? Don't worry though, I understand your money challenges and I am going to discount your investment."

b) Bonus Offer:

"I'm excited to work with you and I know you want to move forward on this. I'm also going to throw in the bonus ________ on top of the discount. The bonus is $________ of free value. If I were able to do that, would that make your decision to move forward easier?"

c) Actual Investment:

"When you register today Jim, I will discount your investment to _______ and I will throw in a free __________. I will do ALL of this for only __________. Does this feel right for you, Jim?" (Or, "Does this sound good?")

d) Get Commitment:

"Are you committed to doing this today, Jim?" (A commitment is stronger than a simple "Yes".)

e) Last Chance Offer:

"I'm offering the discount and the bonus today. I don't know if they will be available in the future. Chances are they may not."

d) Last Minute Ownership:

"Imagine what this is going to do for your __________ (fill in a benefit your client wants). You are making the right decision. Are you committed?"

Help your client to own your product one last time by having him imagine the benefits of it. This subtle Imagineering technique will get him to own your product and his future.

e) <u>Buyer's Remorse</u>:

"You are going to love this program Joe. You made an awesome decision, I promise you."

Make sure you congratulate your client on a great decision so he doesn't change his mind later.

By now you realize the power of Transforming Objections into Assets and you have incredible tools to be a master in sales and influence. Let me leave you with a final story to reinforce the power of this chapter.

Powerful Stories in the Final Countdown:

Have you ever seen the movie "A Time to Kill" with Samuel L Jackson and Matthew McConaughey? I would encourage you to watch the ending of this film. Movies are such a great metaphor for life. In the movie, Matthew is a white lawyer in the south. He is representing Samuel, a black man. Samuel has been accused of murdering two white men. These white men raped and killed his black, ten year old girl. Matthew is trying to get Samuel off on a plea of insanity. Before the closing speeches by the attorneys, Samuel tells Matthew, "You're one of them. I chose you because you're a white attorney. You think like them. YOU ARE THEM. If you want to get me off, you have to think like them!!!!!"

In the closing scene, Matthew does something brilliant. He says, "I want to tell you a story about a little girl who is ten years old. Imagine……"

- Immediately he puts them in the story so they can identify with and relive the experience.
- As a salespreneur, you want to tell your clients stories that they can identify with so they are inspired to take action.

Matthew goes on to tell them this drawn out story with compassion and tremendous feeling. He walks them through the entire scene about the little black girl in exact detail. He talks about how she was raped, her body was soiled, she was hung, used for target practice, urinated on, beaten and thrown off a bridge into the water and left to die. At the end of the scene, there is complete silence in the court room, the eyes of the jury and the other parties are blood shot red. Tears are flowing and hearts have been opened to the tragedy of a little girl. She is no longer someone who died. At this point her presence and the atrocities done to her are in the courtroom. Every single person in the courtroom, even the opposing council is silent. Matthew has evoked the emotion and hearts of everyone.

Now for his final words, "Now imagine she's white."

You will have to watch the ending to see what happens. Once the all white jury saw her as white, they were all able to picture their little girls or granddaughters. You could hear a pin drop in the room. There was no prejudice left in that courtroom, there were only people.

Here is my point as it relates to a salespreneur. Too many times we want people to understand the benefits of our product without putting them in a place where they can feel and see themselves owning the product and experiencing the benefits as if they owned the product already. People make buying decisions on EMOTION. Matthew had the jury experience what happened to that little black girl, rather than just telling them the facts. The secret is he got them to IMAGINE and experience their feelings.

When you get your clients to imagine, they will begin to see themselves and feel themselves having what they want. When you get their other senses involved, you can tap into a part of them that imagines already having it as if it were real. You can tap into their emotion. There are 384 senses that we have as humans and we are very rarely conscious of more than five of them. Get clients to imagine and start using their other senses so you can activate their feelings, which will activate their desire to buy.

All throughout your presentation you should be diffusing objections before they come up. One of the ways to do this is to share powerful stories of other clients who were in a similar situation. When you share a story of someone who is like them, they can immediately identify with that person. Once they identify with that person, they will be able to see themselves doing what that person did. If their objection is "money" you could share a story about how "client x" found a solution to come up with the money and is now living his dream life. Once you share the story, they begin to imagine themselves doing the same thing and now you have yourself a client who is inspired to buy. This is one of the keys to the success of a Master Salespreneur. Once you know your clients' desires and understand their needs, you should do everything you can to INFLUENCE them to buy.

END

In the end, I believe that we are who we see ourselves to be. Each person has a best version of himself. Each salesperson has a best version of who he is. I call it a "Salespreneur." You can define success in sales however you please. You know how you see yourself currently. Perhaps by now, you see yourself how you want to be and more importantly WHO you want to be. Is your Best Salespreneur showing up every day? More importantly is your Best Self showing up every day? If it is, then nothing else matters. If it isn't, then nothing else matters. I have five words for you that sum up this book, "BE YOUR BEST SALESPRENEUR NOW." Live by those words and you will be a Master in Sales and Influence. And now, I have three final questions for you:

1) Who are you?
2) Why do you do what you do?
3) What is your passion?

These are the questions I asked you in the beginning of this book and these are the questions to ponder for a lifetime. Answer them honestly and life will never let you down. For it's not what we do that defines us, it is who we are. Be Your Best Self Now!

Are you committed to challenging the status quo?

Are you committed to being a maverick in the sales industry?

Are you committed to being a leader and change agent?

IF YOU ARE, YOU WILL "NEVER BE CLOSING" AGAIN!

Index

Lightning Source UK Ltd.
Milton Keynes UK
UKHW010339031221
394946UK00008B/434/J